LONDON
UNDER ATTACK
FROM CAESAR TO HITLER

MICHAEL FOLEY

The History Press

To Joseph Kox,
A very special person sadly missed.

I would like to thank Pam Kox for her help in writing this book.

First published 2010

The History Press
The Mill, Brimscombe Port
Stroud, Gloucestershire, GL5 2QG
www.thehistorypress.co.uk

© Michael Foley, 2010

The right of Michael Foley to be identified as the Author of this work
has been asserted in accordance with the Copyrights, Designs and Patents
Act 1988.

British Library Cataloguing in Publication Data.
A catalogue record for this book is available from the British Library.

ISBN 978-07524-5186-2

Typesetting and origination by The History Press
Printed in Great Britain
Manufacturing managed by Jellyfish Print Solutions Ltd

CONTENTS

Other books by Michael Foley

Front-Line Essex
Front-Line Kent
Essex Ready For Anything
Hard As Nails
Front-Line Suffolk
Front-Line Thames
More Front-Line Essex
Essex in the First World War

INTRODUCTION

Although one may consider the position of London as being in the front line of the various conflicts that have overtaken the country throughout history, there would seem to be only a very few occasions when the city has actually been threatened by the forces of some foreign power. In fact the number of threats that occured between the raids of the Vikings in the ninth and tenth centuries and the German air attacks of the First World War would seem to have been minimal. There was undoubtedly a long period when no foreign power attacked the inhabitants of the city at all, despite some coming quite close to the capital, including sorties on a number of occasions by various foes who sailed up the River Thames by ship.

There were, however, numerous times when the fear of a foreign power reaching the city gripped the population of London. There have been even more occasions when it was not only foreigners that the government and the population of London had to fear. When Napoleon threatened to invade the country in the early nineteenth century, those responsible for protecting the city were as worried about the danger from their own population as they were about French troops.

That is all far from the whole story, however. In this long period of what appears to have been a peaceful existence, there were numerous battles that actually took place in London itself. These occurred when the city was often attacked by the armies of its own countrymen. The seemingly peaceful existence of the royal family in the present day was virtually unknown during much of London's history. There were constant periods of political battles between monarchs and parliament, the aldermen of the city and rebel barons. In many cases, the political battles broke out into open violence. The attackers were often the recognised forces of those involved in civil war or the semi-military mobs of those men with a grievance who displayed it with violence against the inhabitants of London.

Even then, the story of conflict in the city is not finished. Since its foundation the city of London has been continuously riven by violence as political and religious differences have driven the population to fight among themselves in large-scale riots. These were often the cause of numerous deaths and injuries to the people and to the property of Londoners.

One often hears of the violence on the streets of London today and wonders how unsafe the city has become. Mention knife crime, robbery, murder and the problems of immigration, the policing of riots and even the rules of 'stop and search' followed by the police, and you could be reading this morning's newspaper. However, these events were just as common – if not more so – before the twentieth century and the emergence of what we now see as 'modern London'.

The episodes in this book will show how London of the past was a much less safe place than it is today. Knife crime in London is not a modern phenomenon at all; the Middle Ages were a time when the rights of lordship were imposed and quarrels between men were settled with a knife or a sword. There was little difference between private or state wars and violence on the city streets has been the norm throughout the past and was not a rare occurrence.

A look into its history will also show how there seems to be nothing new in modern events. The claim that foreigners living in London are better thought of and treated than English citizens could be the headline of one of the tabloid newspapers of today. In fact it was said of foreigners living in London during the reign of Henry VIII and at numerous other times. Often the way foreigners were dealt with was much more severe than what we would expect to see happen today. Outbreaks of robbery in the mid-nineteenth century were openly blamed on the swaggering, stiletto-carrying Italians of Whitechapel, and respected newspapers called for their deportation – all this with no proof of their guilt at all.

The treatment of miners during the violent strikes of the premiership of Margaret Thatcher led to police from London being involved in the violent exchanges. This was also not a modern phenomenon and the same thing had occurred in the past. The recent disputes over the police methods of dealing with demonstrations are also nothing new; they have been going on since the nineteenth century when the police first appeared on the capital's streets.

The position of London as a front line city goes well beyond the few events of foreign war that have reached its limits. The majority of the violence it has seen has come from within and been carried out by its own population or the inhabitants of neighbouring areas. Perhaps this book will make you feel that the London of the present day is not such a dangerous place after all.

www.authorsites.co.uk/michaelfoley

1

ROMAN LONDON

Although some historians like to argue that London existed before the Romans arrived on our shores, there has been little evidence found to prove this. Thornbury, writing in the late nineteenth century in *Old And New London*, suggested that the capital of the Cassivellanus tribe, attacked by Caesar during his invasion, might have been on the spot where London stands today. Walter Armstrong suggests in his 1880s book *The Thames From Its Rise To The Nore*, that the settlement that stood on the site before the Romans arrived was called Llyn-Did and was a Celtic fortified village on the bank of the Wallbrook stream. He also stated that this was the site of the first Roman fort in the area between what is now Mincing Lane and Cannon Street station.

The position of London has been important to almost everyone since the Romans arrived so it is not implausible to suggest that those around before the Romans would have also found it so.

One of the *Time Team* programmes was concerned with digging out a Bronze Age structure on the bank of the Thames at Vauxhall which could have been a home, a jetty or even a bridge – perhaps the first bridge to cross the Thames in what we know as London. The finds of Bronze Age spearheads in the Thames nearby also seem to point to pre-Roman life in the area. The area was described as being just above the tidal head of the river where salt

Roman soldiers must have been common in early London, except when Boudicca arrived to attack in AD 60.

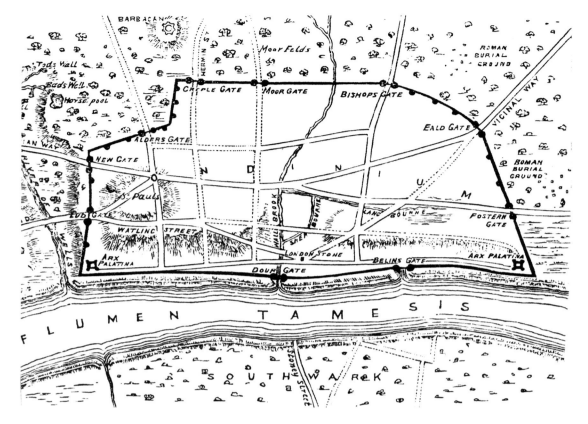

A plan of what Roman London probably looked like.

water met fresh water, which would have been an important site for Bronze Age man. Whether this means that an actual settlement existed on the site is not as clear. It could have been some kind of religious site that was often visited but not settled on.

There is no doubt, however, that London did become an important settlement once the Romans settled in Britain. According to some it was eventually to become a walled town with five gates: Ludgate, Bishopsgate, Aldersgate, Aldgate and Bridgegate. According to Collingwood in *The Archeology of Roman Britain*, the Roman city covered 330 acres and had a population of around 15,000. Much of the Roman wall was built around AD 200 and also included an earlier fort that had been the original Roman military site.

Up until the eighteenth century there were a number of remnants of the Roman wall still standing, but as London grew these were demolished or were built over and were only rediscovered later. In 1763 the remains of a Roman tower were found in Houndsditch while part of the Roman wall was found at Tower Hill in 1852. Bombing during the Second World War also revealed several other remains of the Roman defences.

Part of the Roman wall is visible at Tower Hill although the medieval wall has been built on top of it.

A Dr Stukeley supposedly found evidence of a Roman camp at St Pancras, called the 'Brill', by the old church in 1758. As with many suspected finds, proof seemed to be in short supply and this find was later derided by a Mr B. Woodward in a *Gentleman's Magazine* of 1866.

It seems that the first major conflict that London had to face was the attack by the forces of Boudicca and her Iceni tribe and their allies, including the Trinovantes, in AD 60. The city seems to have been completely destroyed along with the majority of its inhabitants, which at that time almost completely comprised of civilians. The main area of the city then was believed to be around the King's Cross area and the aptly named Battle Bridge. In 1842 a stone was found in the area marked with the symbols of one of the Roman legions that was supposedly part of Gaius Suetonius Paulinus' army which defeated Boudicca, although this battle did not take place in London. Despite Boudicca's destruction, London was to grow again, and stronger and better than it had been before.

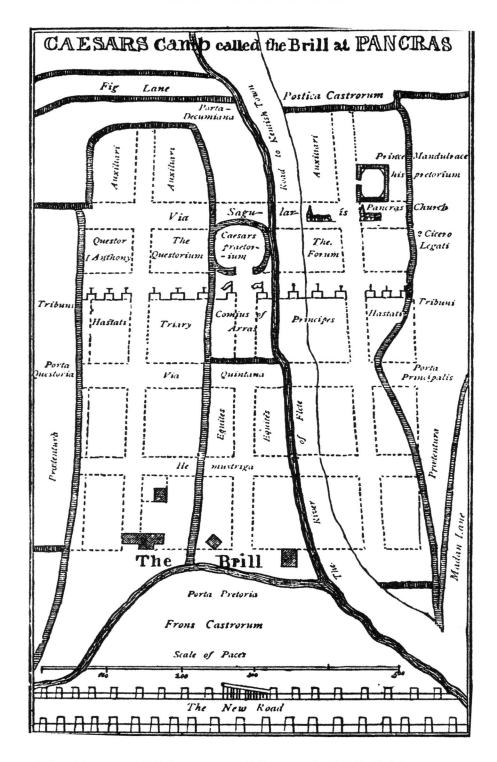

A plan of the supposed Brill Roman camp at St Pancras, as found by Dr Stukeley.

*Part of the old London Wall by the
Museum of London.*

*London Wall and the remains of a Roman fort. A number of remains were found due to bomb damage
in the Second World War.*

A statue of the emperor Trajan near the Roman wall at Tower Hill.

Roman remains found at Billingsgate in the nineteenth century.

Boudicca's statue at the entrance to Westminster Bridge. The chariot also carries her daughters whose treatment was partly responsible for the revolt against the Romans.

There does seem to have been another battle in London during the Roman habitation of Britain. This took place when Carasius declared himself Emperor of Britain and was defeated in 293. His successor was Allectus who was then attacked by Constantius Chlorus to regain control of Britain for Rome in 296. There would seem to have been some fighting in London when Allectus' men fled there from the invading forces. The County Hall ship, found in 1910 when County Hall was being built, was thought to have been one of Allectus' warships as one of his coins was found with the wreckage.

2

SAXON LONDON

After the Romans left Britain there is a period of uncertainty about what happened in London. There are views that the Saxon invaders who came when the Romans left had little use for towns. Surely this does not mean that all the inhabitants of London followed suit and left as well?

The idea of London being deserted during this period seems to be disproved by the *Anglo-Saxon Chronicle*. In AD 449, King Vortigern of Kent asked the Jutish leaders Hengist and Horsa for help against Pictish raiders. The Jutes landed at Ebbsfleet in Kent with their warriors and as more of their countrymen arrived they became an invasion force rather than an ally against the Picts. There was eventually a battle against the Kent people in 457 when the Jutes slew 4,000 of the men of Kent. According to the *Chronicle*, the men from Kent abandoned their lands and fled to the stronghold of London, which would seem to show that the city was still well-occupied and fortified.

From 601, London was the seat of a bishop but at about this time it became part of Mercia. It is a period of uncertainty in the history of the capital that was to last until the arrival of warlike visitors from the north in later centuries. In 825 Egbert of Wessex took London but it was soon to fall into foreign hands as it was in the ninth century that London was to become a city controlled by the Vikings. There were a number of attacks on the city by the Vikings; for example in 842 when a large number of the native population were slaughtered. Then, again, in 851 the Vikings attacked and destroyed most of London. At the same time they captured Canterbury and defeated the Mercians. They were, however, less successful against the kingdom of Wessex. There was another raid in 871, which led to a longer stay and a Viking army marched from Reading and spent the winter in London while making peace with the Mercians.

This period is a confusing one for the history of London. It was never a simple case of the Saxon population of London fighting the invading Vikings. Alliances changed quickly and one group of invaders might become allied to Saxons and find themselves fighting their own countrymen or those from other parts of Scandanavia.

London was, it seems, just another town that seemed to have lost the important position that it had held in Roman times. Eventually the Vikings stopped raiding and settled in the country, controlling much of the east including London. It seems that the town had extended beyond the old Roman walls at this time.

The re-emergence of London's importance to the country came when King Alfred took the town back by force from Viking control in 886 (this was after he had failed to do so in an attack in 882). From this point on it became the chief city of Mercia, then one of the most powerful kingdoms in Britain. Not that this stopped the attacks by the Vikings.

There was an incident between Alfred and the Vikings near London on the River Lea. It seems that the Vikings had fortified the area and had their ships drawn up in the river. There is a legend that Alfred changed the course of the river, trapping the Viking ships. Whatever did happen, it seems that the Vikings were driven off, leaving their ships behind.

In 994, Olaf, King of Norway, and Sweyn, King of Denmark, attacked London with ninety-four ships but were driven off despite their attempts to burn the city down. There was a wooden bridge across the Thames at this time and in 1008 when the Vikings returned they held the crossing. The defenders solved the problem by pulling the structure down.

In 1009 Sweyn had taken most of England but had still failed to capture London and many of his men died in the Thames while trying to cross the river and take the city. He eventually did take control of London, but then died soon after.

London was the scene of further battles between Canute, Sweyn's son, and Edmund Ironside in 1013, until the Viking Canute finally overcame his foe and became King of England. The conflict did not stop there, however, as Edmund successfully returned in 1014. After leaving, Canute returned in 1016 with 160 ships to fight Edmund again. While Canute burned and killed in the countryside, the new king Edmund gathered an army to fight him, which included the garrison of London. Edmund died around this time which was fortunate for his enemy and Canute became king once again.

By the time that Edward the Confessor became king in 1042, Saxon London had evolved from a

A Saxon warrior. The Saxons spent many years defending London against the Vikings.

collection of small huts and the king lived in what was considered great splendour for that time, at Westminster.

The conflict over London was not yet ended however, and recommenced when Harold Godwin was banished from the country after a disagreement with Edward. Harold later returned with his men, sailing up the Thames to London in 1052 where the population cheered his arrival. The population of Southwark decided to let Harold and his men pass through the bridge where they surrounded the king's smaller fleet. Even the king's men did not seem keen to fight Godwin which was part of the reason, no doubt, that Edward decided to welcome him back and even made his son the heir to the throne.

London Bridge was the only bridge in the area for many hundreds of years and was a structure that helped to defend the city on numerous occasions as it blocked the river to those trying to sail up the Thames. On the south bank Southwark became a buffer between those who wished to attack London and the city itself. The defence of the Southwark end of the bridge was usually quite firm. It was only breached during the much later peasants' revolts because someone helped them to get across by opening the gates.

3

NORMAN LONDON

The Saxon reign over London was to be short-lived and, following his victory at Hastings, William the Conqueror was crowned in London in 1066. The coronation was followed by an outbreak of violence that left many of the inhabitants of London dead and part of the city destroyed due, it seems, to a misunderstanding. Trouble at coronations was not an unusual event in the past and after his coronation, William built the Tower of London to keep the town's inhabitants in order. The tower was built close to the old Roman wall by Gundulf, the Bishop of Rochester.

Although Normans were the dominant force after William's success, not all Saxons lost out. Waltheof, Earl of Huntingdon, had opposed William but then joined him and married William's niece Judith. However, despite seemingly being on William's side Waltheof secretly still opposed the new king but his wife Judith informed her uncle of his deeds and he was executed. The earl's castle was later owned by Robert the Bruce who lost it because of his revolt against Edward I.

The next conflict to affect London was after the death of Henry I. The heir of Henry was his daughter, Matilda, whose right to the throne had been seemingly safe when the barons swore allegiance to her. This included Stephen, nephew of Henry and grandson of William,

Norman soldiers. The Normans killed a number of the occupants of London at William the Conqueror's coronation after an outbreak of violence.

One of the gates of the old town. This one was at Aldgate.

ALDGATE.

who then went back on his promise and himself claimed the throne. With the support of the barons he became king in 1135.

Civil war broke out in 1139 between Stephen and Matilda. The population of London supported King Stephen in the civil war but the main conflict took place outside London. The reason for the Londoners' support was mainly because Matilda had abolished some of the liberties previously given to the city by her father, Henry I. There was one particular example of a conflict in the civil war taking place in London. Geoffrey de Mandeville had been the keeper of the Tower of London for Stephen. When Stephen was captured and held prisoner, Matilda arrived in the city and de Mandeville surrendered the tower to her. The

The Tower of London from across the river. The tower has changed enormously since William first built it, with various other monarchs adding to it.

population of the city then rose in revolt and Matilda was driven out of London. With his wife's help, Stephen once more became king. Eventually, however, he was succeeded by Matilda's son, Henry II.

At this time, Old Jewry was already a ghetto in medieval London and persecution of the non-Christian races was the norm. During the reign of King Stephen there were rumours that Jews were using children's blood in their ceremonies. This turned the population against them and led to persecution. Violence against the Jews was to become a regular event throughout medieval history and massacres were quite common. In fact, during the crusades period, the rhetoric of fighting for a Christian god led to the persecution of Jews simply because they were non-Christian. There was widespread violence against the Jews in London when Richard I was crowned. The king had passed a proclamation forbidding Jews to attend the coronation; this was for their own protection due to the bad feeling against them at the time. Richard was in fact hoping to obtain money from them to help finance his crusade. Unfortunately a number of rich Jewish merchants tried to join the festivities at Westminster Hall and were attacked; many of them were beaten to death. A rumour then spread that the king had ordered all Jews to be killed. Many Jewish houses were burned and the inhabitants murdered, often in the name of robbery rather than due to any real anti-Jewish feeling. In many cases killing Jews must have seemed a good way of getting out of repaying debts to them as the Jews were then the main money lenders at this time. The king had obviously not given this order as he then passed laws to protect the Jews, but persecution followed in other parts of the country such as York. Much of this, again, seemed to be provoked more by financial than religious reasons.

By this time the Tower of London had become a prison as well as a fortress and was used for the noblest prisoners in the country. The first of these had been Ralph Flambard, a favourite of William Rufus until the king's death. Flambard escaped from the tower, fled to France and was later pardoned. Important prisoners were treated more like guests in the tower and would pay for what they needed. The poorer prisoners were not as lucky and found themselves confined to the dungeons. This often included a number of Jews who were sent to the tower for what were often ridiculous reasons.

When Richard's brother, John, became king, he used a different approach and taxed the Jews first to gain money before killing them. Also during John's reign another civil war broke out when the rebel barons under Robert Fitzwalter were welcomed into London by the inhabitants. They then destroyed the houses of rich Jews to use the materials to strengthen the walls.

John was responsible for a number of conflicts in London even before he took the throne. In 1191, while King Richard was in Palestine, John and the bishops met in St Paul's Cathedral and accused William de Longchamps, one of the king's regents, of tyranny. Longchamps had paid £3,000 for the position of chancellor but had slowly gained more power in the country and had also become Bishop of Ely. After being excommunicated by the bishops he tried to hold onto power by holding the Tower of London. The population of the city, however, failed to support him and he eventually left the country.

The London population had grown restive during King Richard's absence on the crusade and were turning against the power of the Normans. When Richard returned from captivity a mob gathered and was led by William Fitz Osbert, also known as Longbeard. He asked the king to do something about the great oppression the people were suffering. Longbeard was arrested but then killed one of his captors before taking sanctuary in Bow Church. The church was set on fire to make him come out – which was one way of getting round the sanctuary rules! He was later executed at Tyburn.

When John later became king he agreed to the demands of the rebel barons to sign Magna Carta. He then went back on his word, however, and more civil war followed. To depose John, the barons invited Louis, the eldest son of the King of France, to take the crown of England. Louis was welcomed by the population when he arrived in London in 1216. A few months later, however, and they were happy to see him go after he was paid to leave and Henry III became a child king.

The twelfth century also saw the foundation of the Knights Hospitallers who at first tended the wounded but then became a military organisation similar to the Templars. They were based at Clerkenwell for some time but in 1237 they paraded through the city on their way to the crusades.

The Knights Templar had arrived in 1128, during the reign of Henry I, although they had been formed ten years earlier in Jerusalem by King Baldwin II to protect Christian pilgrims. Their first home was in Holborn but they later built a large monastery near the river, which also included barracks. The knights who trained there played a large part in the crusades and many of them were buried in the area.

Some of the old customs of London still prevailed at this time, such as the Folkmoot, which was a gathering of the people. There had already been conflict between these group meetings and the king, Henry III, in 1240 when

The Knights Templar had a base in London for a number of years.

St John's Gate at Clerkenwell, part of the old base of the knights of St John. A museum of the order is just through the gateway.

the people of London thought that they were not getting their rights, despite the signing of Magna Carta in 1215. These men were later to become the aldermen of the city and the system evolved into the election of a mayor by the fourteenth century. This group would then negotiate with the king to achieve rights for the people of London.

At this time the main royal palace in London was at Westminster. One of the problems causing trouble between the king and the people was the amount of foreigners who gathered around the royal family. The queen's family were the Savoys – who were responsible for the building of the Savoy Palace on the bank of the Thames. There was conflict between the queen's family and the half-brothers of the king as they vied for power and tried to impress their own views on the royal couple. Not only was the foreign influence a problem, but the language spoken in court was French while the population spoke English which further alienated the people from their rulers. The dispute between men such as Roger Bigod, Richard de Clare, Simon de Montfort and the king's half-brothers almost led to a civil war. During the dispute between the people of London and Henry III, watchtowers were built on the city walls while the king was away. When the king returned to the city he forced the removal of the towers.

As early as 1255 the chronicler Matthew Paris complained that London was overflowing with foreigners. There was more trouble in 1258 when the king was forced to recognise parliament with the Provisions of Oxford, instigated by

Simon de Montfort. The following year Henry fell out with his son Edward, later Edward I. Edward allied himself with de Montfort while Richard, the king's brother, came to London with his men and locked the gates against the rebels. Edward and de Montfort fled to St John's Hospital in Clerkenwell. Eventually all sides met in St Paul's and resolved their problems.

However, this did not solve the foreign problem and there were riots in the city and the murder of Italian monks at Cheapside. There was a further uprising by de Montfort in 1261 when Henry managed to overthrow the Provisions of Oxford and later Provisions of Westminster. While Henry occupied the Tower of London, there were more riots in the city. Queen Eleanor opposed the final settlement of Magna Carta and along with her ladies-in-waiting attempted to travel by boat from the tower to Windsor in 1263. A mob on London Bridge dropped stones on the boats, forcing them back to the tower. This event was to have far-reaching effects on the population of London as the queen's son Edward held the insult on his mother against them for some time. In 1263 de Montfort came into the city from the north. The king came from the south and the population of London were for a time undecided as to which side to support. They eventually came down on the side of de Montfort who then took control of London.

The dispute between the king and de Montfort broke out into open war (the Second Barons' War) and they met at the Battle of Lewes. Edward, now on his father's side, led his cavalry against the infantry made up mainly of the population of London. He was so eager to punish them for the insult to his mother that his over-eagerness led to the defeat of the royal army. However, de Montfort was finally defeated at Evesham. His only remaining power base after his defeat was at the Tower of London. Henry wanted revenge on the city and prepared to besiege London. Eventually the population surrendered and the mayor was imprisoned.

In 1267, London was seized once again while the king was absent, this time by Gilbert de Clare, Earl of Gloucester, who was prone to changing his allegiances. Once again the population of London turned against the king and defences were raised around the city.

The disputes that had divided the country and London during Henry's reign were finally settled by the accession of Edward I. He had a long memory, however, and his improvements to the tower were his way of subduing the population. Edward was to spend much of his time away fighting in Wales, France, the Holy Lands and Scotland.

Persecution of Jews, which had taken a backseat during all the civil strife, began again, and by 1275

A fourteenth-century knight with mixed mail and plate armour.

London Bridge was one of the more popular spots for displaying the heads of executed criminals and traitors. Telescopes could be hired to get a better view.

all Jews over the age of seven years old were forced to wear yellow badges. There were anti-Jewish riots and Italians in the city were forced to hide in the tower.

During the time that Edward was away fighting, London became a lawless place with violent games taking place in the streets. Armed gangs roamed the streets offering to settle disputes by attacking people for pay. In 1285 there were riots and prisoners escaped from Newgate. The king, on his return, looked to take control. He enclosed St Paul's Churchyard, which had been where the people assembled and where many disputes began. This was not a popular move. The mayor, Ruxley, resigned because of this and there were widespread demonstrations, during which the king had large numbers of people arrested.

The lawlessness of not only London but the rest of the country was not completely solved – in 1303 the crown jewels were stolen from Westminster. Some of the problems had been caused by the king as Edward had released a number of men from prison as recruits for his army. Many claimed that this lawlessness was the result.

During Edward's reign the London population again rose against the king's foreign favourites. They attacked the king's regent in London, the Bishop of Exeter. He had demanded the keys of the city from the mayor. The crowd seized the bishop and beheaded him.

The reign of Edward's son, Edward II, was not to bring much peace to the capital. As early as 1326 there were serious riots in London that were partly to blame for destroying the government of Edward II. The mobs were supporting his wife, Queen Isabella, and her lover Mortimer, who were more popular than the king. Edward was finally forced to abdicate in favour of his son aged fourteen but it was Mortimer and Isabella who really then held power.

Edward's reign was short and unpopular. The French Isabella soon found out that Edward preferred men. It was Isabella and Mortimer who took the throne from Edward. There was some level of royal revenge, however, as when Isabella's son Edward III came to power, he had Mortimer executed.

4

LONDON BECOMES MORE ENGLISH

There had been a change in opinion by the time of Edward III. When he came to power in 1327, England was much more English than it had been in previous reigns. The English dislike of foreigners now included the French with whom they had previously been so well connected. Although the nobility may still have spoken French, English had by this time become the main language in most areas of society.

The dislike of the French also led to numerous wars. There was widespread panic in 1338 when it was expected that the French were about to not only attack the towns along the lower Thames but London itself. The tower had been strengthened along the river over the previous two years and defences were quickly put in place for the rest of London. Wooden piles were driven into the river bed to stop ships landing, artillery and other weapons were stored at the Guildhall and the gates to the city were guarded at all times. At the time England had no permanent navy and had to hire ships from foreigners. English ships that sailed from London had to do so in convoys. They would also be protected by ships from the Cinque Ports.

At this time Southwark was still free of the jurisdiction of the city. Because of this it became a haven for criminals who only had to cross the bridge to gain sanctuary. Then, in 1327, Edward granted the Manor of Southwark to the city of London, which supposedly put an end to the sanctuary. In reality this was still difficult to enforce.

In 1340 Edward III was forced to leave the Low Countries and leave his wife there as a hostage. He had to beg parliament for money to continue his war and began to raise money himself by fining as many people as possible. Trials were held everywhere and always ended in large fines for trivial incidents. These methods were not popular in London and this led to riots on Tower Hill. One of the king's loudest critics at the time was Archbishop Stratford, preaching from the safety of Canterbury Cathedral.

Another form of attack was visited on not only London but also the whole country in 1348 and it was not from any foreign power; it was the Black Death. The plague was to strike a number of times during the century and is believed to have killed between 30-60 per cent of the population of Europe. One of the advantages for the poor of the country was that working men became so scarce that they were in a strong position and the feudal ties that had bound them to the land were relaxed.

There were a number of large houses in the city at this time that were owned by members of the aristocracy. A number of them were built on the banks of the Thames and covered large areas of land. One of these was the Savoy Palace and was later owned by John of Gaunt.

The war in Europe against France was still continuing and the guilds of London turned out in huge numbers to welcome the return of the Black Prince, the son of Edward III, when he returned from his victory at the Battle of Poitiers in 1356. The crowds were so large that it took the prince hours to travel the distance between London Bridge and Westminster. The prince did not return home empty-handed and the Savoy Palace was used to hold King John of France who was taken prisoner at the battle. John was later sent to the tower.

By 1370 the curfew bells were rung at a number of churches. These were St Mary le Bow, All Hallows, St Brides and St Giles. The sound of Bow Bells has been said to have meant something to the inhabitants of the city throughout history as anyone born within their sound is said to be a cockney. Even as early as Norman times, Bow Bells meant something. When they were rung at 9.00 p.m. it was the sound of the beginning of the Norman curfew. Church bells were the means by which the city was ruled. While the main city gates were closed at sunset, at the sound of the curfew bell the wicket gates were then closed. Twelve armed men then guarded the gates – during the Peasants' Revolt this increased to twenty.

Between May and July 1381, the Peasants' Revolt under Wat Tyler and John Ball took place. One of the reasons for this was that the poor were worried that the nobility would try to take back the feudal powers that had been relaxed during the Black Death. They also objected to being forced to work two days a week for the church and, of course, they were against the poll tax. Ball would hold meetings after services on a Sunday at which he would preach that all men are equal and should have equal rights. There are some who believe that the idea behind the revolt was strongly based on a belief in the tales of Robin Hood who was loyal to the king but against corruption. It would seem that the character and stories about the outlaw were known to most people, even those who could not read.

The attack on the city by Tyler's men was aimed at the Richard II's treacherous advisors rather than the king himself, who was at the time only fourteen years old. The mob was let into the city by sympathisers who opened the gates on the bridge allowing them to cross the river into London. The rioters supposedly destroyed the Savoy Palace, released the prisoners in the London prisons and occupied the tower. There is also some doubt about whether this version is true and some believe that it was actually the population of London who destroyed the Savoy Palace before the rebel mob had even entered the city. John of Gaunt, who owned the Savoy Palace at the time, was unpopular with Londoners, as he had been blamed for the poor results of the war in France and for encouraging foreigners to play such an important part in the life of the city.

It was the king's advisors that they were after and the mob took the Archbishop of Canterbury, Simon Sudbury, from the tower and executed him. Wat Tyler then went to meet the king at Smithfield to discuss the situation. He was supposedly then killed by Sir William Walworth, the mayor of the time. After this, the revolt petered out and the rebels began to return home.

After Tyler's uprising there was suspicion against fishmongers in the city and for a short period, fishmongers were barred from becoming Mayor of London. This was partly due to frauds taking place at Billingsgate. It was also suspected that Walter Sybell, a spokesman for the Fishmongers Company, was the one responsible for letting Tyler and his mob into the city. Fishmongers Hall later had a statue erected there of William Walworth, perhaps as a way of showing their support for the city rather than Tyler.

Smithfield was an area of London that was to see many deaths apart from that of Tyler. As well as being a jousting site in the Middle Ages it also became an execution place. Henry VIII burnt those who didn't agree with his taking over the church there. Queen Mary later burnt Protestants there and then Elizabeth burnt Catholics on the same spot. It must have become confusing at times as to who was the enemy to be burnt!

In 1386 there was another plot hatched against the king's advisors, at Hornsey Park. This one, however, was not among the poor. The plotters included the Duke of Gloucester, the Earl of Arundel, the Earl of Warwick and others. They marched on London to oppose Richard II and to try to force him to dismiss his two favourite ministers, the Earl of Suffolk and Robert, Duke of Ireland.

There was a very famous joust held in London in 1390, perhaps intended as a means of deflecting the anger of those who were against the king. It was held between the champion of England, Lord John Welles, and the champion of Scotland, Sir David de Lindsay. The place where the joust was held was very unusual; it was on London Bridge. It was perhaps one of the highlights of an unhappy reign by the king.

Trouble continued for Richard when his banished cousin Bolingbroke returned while he was in Ireland. Bolingbroke gathered an army and marched on London, which he took. On Richard's return, the king was taken prisoner and held in London. Richard was then executed in the tower and Bolingbroke became King Henry IV.

When crowds gathered in London they were not always the result of uprisings against the king; on some occasions the population turned out to greet great victories. One of the most elaborate celebrations of the Middle Ages was the return of the king after the Battle of Agincourt in 1415. It was a month after the

There were a number of sites in London where executions took place. Smithfield was one of those popular for burning at the stake.

battle that the king, Henry V, came home so there had been plenty of time to prepare for it. The mayor and a number of aldermen actually went out and met the king at Blackheath. The king never brought his whole army but a few chosen followers including a number of French prisoners (there could have been many more prisoners if the king had nor ordered the slaughter of the French prisoners during the battle). Large towers had been built and enormous figures stood along the route to the tower, which the king passed, accompanied by the clergy and watched by the population of London.

One of the prisoners taken at Agincourt was Charles, Duke of Orleans. Unlike other important prisoners, Charles was not ransomed – Henry V thought that he was too valuable and he was to remain a prisoner for twenty-five years, many of these being spent in the Tower of London.

Despite Henry's success in France, his reign was not without trouble at home. A former friend of the king, Sir John Oldcastle, was a follower of Wycliffe, a religious dissident, and despite his friendship with the king was imprisoned in the tower. He then escaped and was adopted as a leader of the Lollard movement which was what Wycliffe's followers were known as. When a large meeting of the Lollards took place in St Giles Fields, the king had the city gates shut to stop them escaping and attacked the gathering with his knights. Many of those at the meeting died while others were imprisoned. Oldcastle retained his freedom, however, for some time, but was eventually caught and was burned.

Henry's son became Henry VI at the age of eight. There was an uprising of a very strange kind in the reign of Henry VI, which also originated at Hornsey Park where an earlier revolt had begun. The Duchess of Gloucester, Robert Bolingbroke and Thomas Southwell attempted to consume the king by witchcraft. Bolingbroke was executed at Tyburn for his part in the plot while Southwell later died in the tower. The duchess was lucky to survive, but forced to perform penance on the streets by walking through the town wearing a white sheet and carrying a candle.

Henry's reign was to also see a revolt that at one point led to the loss of London. There was a revolt in 1450 when Jack Cade and his followers gathered at Blackheath for a month. The area was to be a popular one with dissident groups. They were against what they saw as a weak king and high taxes. Cade's followers were joined by not only the poor but also some knights and other members of the nobility. The gates to London Bridge were closed to Cade but they attacked the bridge. Despite the guns from the tower firing on them, they eventually managed to cross the bridge. The mob then marched on the tower to make their demands. Several of the king's counsellors were captured and beheaded. The mob then set about looting the city.

The rebellion had been supported by many of the population of London but they eventually grew tired of the violence. Cade and his men returned across the bridge for the night. The following day the citizens of London decided enough was enough and held the bridge, preventing them from crossing, no doubt unwilling to suffer the same experience again. The defenders of the bridge were led by Captain Matthew Gough who had fought in France with Henry V. The fight lasted for hours with many of the inhabitants of the houses on the bridge dying after the rebels set fire to their homes. Eventually, Cade's men were driven off the bridge. They then decided that the rebellion was over and went home with the loot they had stolen. However, not all of the rebels lived to enjoy their gains. Cade died on his way back to London after being wounded in the fight to capture him. Many others were executed in their own towns.

The problems suffered by Henry VI seemed endless. In 1452 the heir to the throne, the Duke of York, returned from Ireland where he had been sent and raised an army against the king. The king raised his own army in London and this led to a stand off outside the city. The king agreed with some of York's demands but then did not carry them out. York's popularity then waned.

The king's problems did not end there, however. Henry VI was to have a mental breakdown in 1453 and York finally became regent. Henry had by this time had an heir, Edward. When the king regained his senses, the Wars of the Roses broke out with York winning and becoming Edward IV. By this time Henry had gone mad again and was eventually captured and locked in the tower.

There was a further successful uprising due to Henry's wife and he was returned to the throne. This only lasted for six months before Edward returned and won back the crown while Henry's son died at the Battle of Tewkesbury. Henry was returned to the tower where he died shortly after. There was suspicion that his death was not due to natural causes and that he had been murdered by Edward.

In 1471, while the forces of Henry and Edward were fighting in the north, the so-called Thomas the Bastard of Fauconberg attacked London, mooring his ships by the tower. He was a supporter of Henry and was the son of Lord Fauconberg, one of the Warwick family. He hoped to free Henry from the tower. The city was barricaded and the bridge became the main battleground. Unable to cross, a number of Fauconberg's men traversed the river in boats and broke into the city, only to be defeated. The forces were eventually driven off by the population of the city and slain in large numbers as they fled. The defence of London had been organised by the sheriff, John Crosby.

Blackheath was once again a popular spot for revolting bands of men when, in 1497, there was a gathering there of Cornishmen led by Thomas Flamank and Michael Joseph. The large Cornish mob had come from the West Country to rebel against the taxes imposed on Cornwall by Henry VII to pay for his war against the Scottish. The population of London was sent into a widespread panic by the Cornish gathering and the royal family moved into the tower for their own protection. Unfortunately for the Cornishmen, the king's large army that had been gathered to fight the Scots was quickly recalled to London. The king's army then attacked the Cornish mob at Blackheath and, despite some success with archers at Deptford Bridge, the Cornish mob was soon overcome with resulting widespread slaughter. The ringleaders were then taken and executed.

5

TUDOR LONDON

During the reign of Henry VIII there was yet another dispute involving foreigners. The problem was with foreign moneylenders who were living in London. The Lombards were already unpopular when one of them, Francis de Bard, seduced a man's wife. Not content with taking his wife, he also took the man's belongings. The husband tried to get his belongings back, but lost the court case – it wasn't stated whether he wanted his wife back as well. It was later reported that de Bard was boasting about his conquest; the result was that when the Easter sermons were read out at St Mary's Spital and at St Paul's Cross there was further condemnation of the influence of foreigners. The sermons were part of an open-air event which was attended by the mayor and other important people. One sermon, by a Dr Bell, stated that foreigners had more liberty in the country than Englishmen. He then went on to call for Englishmen to defend themselves and hurt aliens. There followed an outbreak of quarrels with foreigners on the streets of London in April 1513 and rumours were spread that May Day and the associated celebrations would be the spark to cause an outbreak of violence against foreigners. Servants were forbidden to go out on May Day but a large crowd still gathered on the streets and attacked the homes of foreigners living in London. More than 300 of the mob were arrested and Dr Bell was sent to the tower for his inflammatory sermon. Thirteen of the prisoners were hanged but the rest were then pardoned by the king.

The defence of the country became more organised under Henry. The bow was still the main form of weapon used by the people and Shoreditch was used as a practice ground for archers. After one archery competition at Windsor, the king conferred the mock title of the Duke of Shoreditch on the competition's winner. The man honoured with the title was named Barlow and after this he led archers to the Hoxton, Islington and Stoke Newington butts. Henry also decreed that every father had to give his son a bow at the age of seven with which he could practice. There were protests when landowners tried to plant hedges on land used for archery practice as it interfered with the shooting. It seems that archery took precedence over land ownership.

Sir Thomas More lived at Chelsea during Henry's reign and had part of his home converted into a prison for heretics. One of those to be held there was a lawyer, John Baynham, who held the doctrines of Wycliffe. The Lollards had already been persecuted in earlier reigns and Baynham was often whipped in the garden and was eventually burnt at Smithfield, ironic given that a few years later and the whole country would be forced to subscribe to Protestantism of which Wycliffe and the Lollards were early pioneers.

Henry's actions in taking over the church and closing monasteries (the Dissolution) in the 1530s was not accepted by all the population without opposition. The result of Henry's actions meant that whereas everyone in the country had previously been a Catholic they were suddenly Protestants. There had been no choice in the matter. A large force, inspired by monks who had lost their livelihood because of Henry's action, gathered in the north of the country. Eventually around 30,000 men marched on London in support of the Pope and the monasteries. The dispute died out, however, before there were any serious conflicts and the leaders were kept in the Tower of London and were later executed.

After Henry's death there was a period of uncertainty when religion was the biggest cause of dispute in the country. The safety of Catholics and Protestants could change overnight depending on the country's ruler. The actions by Henry were to be one of the biggest causes of violence and death in the country over the next few hundred years as each side denounced and burnt the other depending on who was in power. Although the endless executions owing to religious differences may seem extreme to us today, looked at in the value of life in those times it is quite understandable. During the Tudor period the death sentence could be imposed for the theft of property worth one shilling. A shilling may have been worth much more then but it still seems a very cheap price for a life.

It was this dispute between the followers of Rome and the English Church that was to lead to another revolt in 1554 when Sir Thomas Wyatt arrived at London with a large force prepared to do battle to stop the marriage of Queen Mary to Philip of Spain. This was to stop the country once again becoming part of the Catholic faith under Spanish influence – not that the queen needed any foreign input to persecute Protestants. The mob attacked London Bridge but was driven off by the guns in the tower. Wyatt's force then went away and attempted to cross the river at Kingston where there was another bridge. This had, however, been destroyed by locals. They did manage to rebuild the bridge and cross the river and one skirmish took place at Hay Hill near Berkeley Square between Wyatt's men and the army. The rebels were eventually stopped at the Ludgate and finally surrendered at Temple Bar. After his execution, Wyatt's head was set upon a gallows at Berkeley Square.

When Elizabeth I became queen, the Protestant faith once more came into the ascendancy. In 1567 Mary Queen of Scots fled to her cousin Elizabeth for protection after trouble in Scotland. She then became an attraction for Catholic dissidents who tried to involve her in their plots. This eventually led to her death at the hands of the executioner.

In 1585 it became treason for a Catholic priest to be in the country and it became a felony to harbour one. The King of Spain was fed up with the anti-

Catholic feeling in England and decided to invade using the Spanish Armada in 1588 and was famously repelled.

The reign of Elizabeth was not only one of intrigue and killing. It saw the beginning of exploration and the acquisition of colonies that led to the foundation of the British Empire. One of these ventures actually set out from London itself when, in 1576, Martin Frobisher, later to be a commander in the defeat of the Armada, set out from Blackwall to find the North-West Passage.

Public executions were not only frequent but also very popular in London at the time and there were Law Days when up to thirty people could be hanged. A German visitor to the city in 1599 noticed that there were gallows everywhere. The heads of those who were executed often found themselves impaled on spikes on London Bridge.

A little less brutal, the popularity of the theatre had grown in Elizabeth's reign and many of them had sprung up in Southwark. At one point they were banned in London as anything that attracted large crowds was seen as a threat to law and order. The queen liked theatre, however, and because of her royal patronage they were allowed to continue.

During the reign of Elizabeth I, the area of Westminster was mainly marshland and apart from the abbey and Millbank Palace, there were very few buildings. Hyde Park was at the time a hunting ground owned by the royal family. It was also used as a review ground for troops as early as 1569 when the Queen's Pensioners paraded on horseback in armour, ready to be inspected by the queen.

In 1579 Tothill Fields was used as a training ground for archers. The artillery ground in Artillery Lane, Bishopsgate, was also used by crossbowmen. It was later used by the Tower of London gunners for gunnery practice and by the Trained London Bands up to 1585. Although the practice of archery had declined somewhat by Elizabeth's reign, it was still a well-followed activity. Grub Street was still full of fletchers who supplied the archers with their arrows. Under James I from 1603, Moorfields was in use as a new artillery ground. It was bigger than the old grounds at Spitalfields and could used by larger forces – the old grounds had become too small.

There were hopes that the accession of James, whose mother had been a Catholic, would have led to a more lenient attitude towards the religion. This turned out to be wrong and led to one of the most famous Catholic intrigues, the Gunpowder Plot of 1605. The popular view of how the plot was discovered was that Guy Fawkes was found in the cellars of the Houses of Parliament with a stack of gunpowder as he was about to light the fuse. This, however, was contested in a work by Francis Edwards who translated the narrative of Oswald Tesimond. Edwards claims that the plot was actually based in a house rented by the plotters whose cellars were situated beneath parliament. It was in these cellars where the gunpowder was stored, not in the actual cellars of Parliament. He also claims that the plot was discovered after one of the group sent a letter to a friend who was due to sit in parliament that day, warning him not to go. The person who received the letter then alerted the authorities and the plot was discovered.

6

CIVIL WAR

There were events during the reign of Charles I that bore a resemblance to the behaviour of the Nazis in the Second World War who burnt books that did not agree with their views. The cross at Cheapside had been pulled down in 1643 due to its popish leanings and in 1645, crucifixes, popish pictures and books were burnt on the site. Despite this, Charles was obviously in sympathy with the Catholic religion and the Duke of Buckingham arranged his marriage to the Catholic Henrietta Maria. Buckingham was then stabbed to death on 28 August by a Protestant, John Felton, who had a personal grudge against the duke but expected his actions to be well received owing to the duke's pro-Catholic connections.

Charles I did not court favour with his better-off subjects when he seized all the money from the Royal Mint, supposedly as a loan. Up until this time, the mint had been used as a bank by the rich. After this, the Goldsmith's Company became the city's main bankers.

After the dissolution of parliament by the king there were rumours passing around the city that Lambeth Palace would be burnt, hopefully with William Laud, later accused of treason and beheaded, inside. In 1640 there was an assembly of apprentices at St George's Fields with this object in mind. The Southwark militia were called out but left the scene at midnight while there was still a large crowd gathered. The crowd then went to Lambeth Palace but Laud was not there. Some damage was done to the gardens. A witness to this scene was the diarist John Evelyn. He said that at this time London was subject to frequent disorder and that the Bishop of Canterbury's palace at Lambeth was attacked by a rabble from Southwark. Obviously Evelyn was not on the side of the rebellion! The crowds that gathered in the city with the object of causing trouble often came from outside the old city walls. London had by this time expanded and was surrounded by a sprawling, low-class suburb over which the city authorities had little control.

The dispute between the king and his subjects led to more extreme events than trouble on the streets. In 1641 the Earl of Stafford was imprisoned in the Tower of London against the king's wishes. In May the king sent troops to rescue him but they were thwarted by the lieutenant of the tower. This led to more crowds taking to the streets in protest at the king's actions and the wife of the king was often attacked in the streets for being a Catholic. The trial of Stafford took place in Westminster Hall and was described by Evelyn as 'there being no human law that he broke so a new one was made.' Evelyn then witnessed Stafford's execution on Tower Hill, describing it as the separation of the wisest head in England from his shoulders.

Charles had already upset the Scottish by introducing the use of an Anglican style liturgy. He then upset parliament over everything, including trying to raise endless taxes and then by attempting to arrest five members of parliament in the house. After further unsuccessful attempts to arrest the men in the city the following day, the king left London. By this time London was in uproar and there were armed men in boats along the Thames. Captain Skipton, who had been a captain of the artillery ground, was given a new role as major general of militia and put in command of the Trained London Bands. There had been an increase in the popularity of military literature since the early 1640s as men became involved in the dispute and no doubt were expecting to have to fight at some stage. They soon got their wish as the Civil War between parliament and the king broke out.

Hyde Park was used as a muster ground for troops again when the Trained London Bands gathered there. The bands were at one point loyal to the king. They then turned their support to parliament and in 1642 they joined Lord Essex at Brentford to fight against the Royalist forces.

The belief early in the war was that Prince Rupert was about to attack and sack the city of London. The first defences that the town had were no more than chains stretched across roads, but this soon progressed to more secure defences and in 1642 Tothill fields was the site of batteries and defences to protect London from the Royalist army. Many of the suburbs were fortified, including a redoubt

and battery on Constitution Hill. The area was no stranger to conflict having been a popular spot for fighting duels, although now the threat of much larger action hung over the area. The west end of Piccadilly was also fortified by Londoners against an attack by Charles. Stepney was also fortified. The London defences eventually stretched for 11 miles around the city and were built on both sides of the river. These defences included twenty-two forts mostly joined by earthworks. They were known as the 'Lines

The Trained London Bands were to prove to be a disciplined and effective fighting force, especially during the Civil War.

The pike had been a useful weapon for a number of years and despite the widespread use of firearms during the Civil War it was still a common weapon.

of Communication' and their construction led to the destruction of a number of private properties. Most of the work was carried out in 1643 by volunteers from the population of London.

The biggest danger that the city faced was after the Battle of Edgehill in October 1642, which was essentially a stalemate between the two sets of forces. When the Parliamentary forces headed north after the battle, the road to London was left clear for the Royalists. The king, however, refused to attack the capital.

There seemed to be a difference of opinion as to the advantages of building defences around the town. The Royalist Prince Rupert was very much in favour of them while Sir John Meldrum, a supporter of the Parliamentary side, thought they would do no more than invite an attack. Why a well-defended town would be more likely to be attacked than one with no defences seems a strange opinion to hold.

The majority of the citizens of London seemed to have helped with the earthworks and were organised by Isaac Pennington, the mayor. Thousands of people helped to erect batteries, redoubts and forts. These were people of all classes and parades were held led by drummers to encourage volunteers join in and to help raise the defences. These were mainly ditches and earthen banks linking a number of forts. One of these forts was at St Pancras near Brill Farm, now the site of the old St Pancras church. The people even worked on Sundays and it is believed that up to 20,000 helped build the defences. All were working for nothing apart from rations. The lines had another result in that the security that they seemingly gave encouraged the citizens of the city to stay there and

Not everyone in London supported parliament during the war. Two Royalist sympathisers planned an uprising and were caught. Tomkins and Challoner were then executed.

encouraged businessmen to continue trading in London. The defence work was paid for by a tax on the suburbs, which amounted to £12,000 in 1643. The following year the areas had to pay a monthly tax of Westminster £616, Tower Hamlets £419 and Southwark £369.

Despite the security that the defences seem to have given the city, there were some dangers. In 1643 two men named Tomkins and Challoner were living in Holborn. They had a plan to help the king, which included securing the king's children and seizing members of parliament such as Pym and Colonel Hampden. They also planned to arrest the mayor and, with a committee of the militia, capture part of the city's defences and let in a Royalist force of 3,000 men. The conspirators were to wear white ribbons on their arms to show their allegiance. Tomkins' servant informed on them and they were arrested and later hanged at Fetter Lane.

Although London itself may not have been attacked there were several skirmishes nearby. There was supposedly evidence found of a battle at Knightsbridge and Cromwell's bodyguard were supposed to have been put up at the Rose and Crown Inn. There was also a battle at Brentford, which was a separate village at the time.

The Parliamentary army during the Civil War had begun to look more like the armies we know today with a recognised uniform.

What is now West London was then a number of villages and Fulham and Putney were of vital importance during the war. In 1647 Cromwell was camped at Putney and a bridge of boats was placed across the Thames in the area and was fortified at either end.

Despite the religious zealousness at the time of the Civil War, it was Cromwell who first began to show toleration towards the Jews. Along with everyone else they were a source of finance. The civil companies in London also had to pay

London was surround by defences during the Civil War. These consisted mainly of earthworks connecting a number of forts This was the fort at St Pancras.

towards the costs of the war. In 1645 the Grocers Company paid £50 a week to support the troops, £6 for city defences and £8 for the wounded soldiers. They had to sell £1,000-worth of plate to find the money. They were later asked for £4,500 for arms and the defences of the city. Grocer's Hall was also used to hold parliamentary committee meetings and in 1648 Fairfax wanted to billet his troops in the hall.

It was 1647 when Cromwell and Ireton heard of a royal plan to kill them. They disguised themselves as soldiers and stayed at the Blue Boar Inn at Holborn waiting for the messenger bringing the orders for the deed. They found the papers hidden in the messenger's saddle, which included letters from the king to the Queen of France, planning their murder. It was this plot that had a part in leading to the king's death.

In 1647 Fairfax marched his army into Southwark but the gates on the bridge were shut against him. There was some dispute between the army and those who controlled London who did not want to be ruled by the army. No one manned the defences to oppose him. The army eventually marched into the city and, after gathering in Hyde Park, moved out again. Not only was there dispute between the army and the people but there were also divisions within the army itself. A group of Levellers called for democracy and religious tolerance. In 1647 they met with the army commanders at St Mary's church in Putney but their demands were refused.

In August 1651, 14,000 men were present at the gathering of the Trained Bands of London at Tothill Fields. The following month, the Battle of Worcester was fought and around 1,200 Scottish prisoners were gathered in the fields from the battle. Many of them were sold as slaves to the West Indies but many who did not survive were buried in the area.

Cromwell was often in danger during his time in control of the country. During one event in King Street, Westminster, Cromwell's coach became stuck in the crowd. Lord Broghill saw someone come from a cobbler's shop. He drew his sword and shouted a warning as the man coming out of the shop was holding a sword. The man was thought to be an officer from Ireland.

The period after the Civil War was definitely not one of peace. Many poor groups of people had set up homes on former royal lands but these were then sold off to those who could afford them. One example of this was at Enfield Chase, which was then just outside London. An ex-army officer bought the land and began to farm the area. The locals who had settled the site then let their cattle encroach onto the owner's fields, ruining his crops. The owner then recruited some soldiers to put a stop to this but they were attacked by a huge crowd, which led to deaths and serious wounds on both sides.

In 1657 the control of the military and the puritans over many aspects of life was shown when John Evelyn went to London on Christmas Day and attended a religious service in a chapel in the house he was staying in. The house was surrounded by soldiers and the congregation arrested. They were told that celebrating Christmas was no longer allowed. The soldiers also suspected that prayers had been said for Charles Stuart. When the congregation claimed they prayed for all lawful kings they were charged with praying for the King of Spain, the enemy of England and a papist. Most of them were eventually released.

When Cromwell died in 1658 the route to his final resting place in Westminster Abbey was lined with soldiers. Cromwell's son Richard took over his role as Lord Protector but was not the same type of man that his father had been. The country was heading towards anarchy by the time a strong man did take control. General Monck had been Governor of Scotland since subduing the country in 1651. In 1660 he marched his army down to London and restored parliament to its old status. Monck was also instrumental in the restoration of the king.

"IT'S ALL VERY WELL, MR. CROMWELL: BUT YOU CAN'T LODGE HERE."

There was some dispute in the nineteenth century as to whether a statue of Cromwell was suitable, as shown in this cartoon of the time.

Opinion on Cromwell obviously changed later as this statue that now stands outside parliament shows.

Conflict had still not come to an end however. There was a battle in 1661 between the Trained London Bands and the Fifth Monarchy Men, a group led by Thomas Venner. The monarchy men had tried to unseat Cromwell in 1657 and again attempted to fight the newly restored royal government of Charles II in 1661. The group believed in a passage from the bible that predicted five kingdoms, the last of which would make way for a new kingdom on earth. The group were responsible for a number of murders in London but were smaller in number than they were thought to be and did not present such a serious threat as many were led to believe. They were eventually found where they were hidden in Caen Woods, between Hampstead and Highgate. Some were killed but many were taken prisoner. Venner was later executed.

7

ROYAL LONDON AGAIN

The Trained London Bands were again paraded in Hyde Park just after the restoration and numbered 18,000. In 1662 the Life Guards who had been formed in Holland were also reviewed in Hyde Park and were much more colourful in uniform than Cromwell's men had been. A review of the guards in 1664 was mentioned by Samuel Pepys who said that they numbered 4,000. The Duke of Monmouth became the colonel of the guards and in 1682 they were again reviewed by Charles II and his guest, the Sultan of Morocco.

The plague was a danger in London at this time and had returned in 1665/6 and killed around 20 per cent of the population of the city. It had been a regular visitor in the previous sixty years or so of the century. In 1603 it killed 38,000, in 1625 30,000 died and 1636 it was the cause of 100,000 deaths. Many people left the city during the outbreaks of sickness, including the royal family. In 1665 the lord mayor Sir John Lawrence supposedly stayed in the city to perform his duties, but carried them out while enclosed in a glass box.

Highgate had become a popular place to live in the seventeenth century. This was partly due to the Lord Protector. Cromwell House in the area had been built by Cromwell in 1630 for General Ireton who married Cromwell's daughter. The staircase was carved with military figures, which was well suited to its occupant. By this time firearms

The staircase of Cromwell House, home of Ireton with its military figures on the posts.

The monument to the Great Fire of London. It originally featured a plaque blaming the fire on Catholics.

and artillery had become the main weapons of the forces. Although there were laws passed later to limit the amount of gunpowder that could be kept in the capital for safety reasons, in 1649 they were not in force. It was no surprise then that accidents occurred, like the one in a chandler's shop near the churchyard of All Hallows, Barking, in Tower Street. Twenty-seven barrels of powder exploded, ruining several houses and causing a number of deaths. As the use of gunpowder and artillery grew, sites used to test the weapons were moved further out of the capital.

The Great Fire of London in 1666 was an attack on the city of a different kind. After the fire, thousands of people camped on Highgate Hill. The poor camped there also had affluent neighbours. Lauderdale House in Highgate had a history of famous inhabitants and was the home of the Earls of Lauderdale. The changing face of high status families was evident in the family history as one of the earls gave Charles I to parliament but then later became a royalist under Charles II and persecuted the Covenanters. The house was also the home of Nell Gywnne before it eventually became a convalescent home for St Bartholomew's Hospital.

Following the Great Fire, an even more catastrophic event was to befall London the following year. The wars with the Dutch had been an ongoing concern but in 1667 the Dutch fleet sailed unhindered into the Thames itself.

The old Admiralty buildings from where control of the British navy was operated through many of the conflicts of the past.

They took the partly completed fort at Sheerness and then moved up to the Medway to attack the shipyard at Chatham. The defences that were supposed to protect the important sites on the Thames were found sorely lacking. Many of the weapons at these sites were out of date or useless and some even had the wrong size ammunition for the weapons. The men manning them often ran away rather than standing to fight the invader. Upnor Castle, dating back to Elizabeth I, was one of the only defences to put up anything like a good show against the Dutch. A number of the navy's most powerful warships were captured by the Dutch, such as the *Royal Charles*, the pride of the English navy.

London was thrown into panic by the attack. One of the few defensive structures left on the Thames between the Dutch fleet and the capital was Tilbury Fort, which was also sadly out of date and almost decrepit. It seemed that if the Dutch sailed on London nothing could be done to stop them. The panic in the city was described by writer and diarist John Evelyn who himself sent many of his belongings away into safety. He feared that the Dutch would come into London and burn all the ships on the Thames. As he described it, 'Everybody were flying, none knew where or whither.' Strangely, the Dutch decided against going any further up-river and returned back down the Thames towards the sea where they attempted to take Landguard Fort at Felixstowe, which protected Harwich harbour. They were beaten off by the garrison at the fort and, although they threatened further along the Suffolk coast, they seemed to have lost their nerve and there were no further serious attacks. The inadequate defences of the Thames were rectified after this with a number of new and updated defences built along the river to defend the waterborne route into the heart of the country. Tilbury Fort was completely redesigned and rebuilt.

Although there was constant violence in London, the power of the courts to deal with those responsible was not always based on legal rules. William Penn was the son of an admiral in the navy who later went on to found the state of Pennsylvania in America. In 1667, however, he was arrested while attending a meeting of the Quakers. He was tried at the Old Bailey and one of the judges was the lord mayor. Penn was charged with meeting with force of arms to the terror of his majesty's subjects. Penn had legal training and easily disproved the charges which so annoyed the mayor that he told the court officials to stop Penn's mouth. When Penn was found not guilty by the jury, the mayor sent the jury to Newgate until they decided to return the verdict that he wanted. They were eventually released on the orders of the Lord Chief Justice.

The destruction of St Paul's Cathedral in the Great Fire had been a major blow to the city. St Paul's churchyard had always been more than just a churchyard; it had been a place to meet and a public amenity and this was one of the reasons that rebuilding the cathedral was so important. It was also a sign that London was becoming a famous city that needed a great cathedral. Sir Christopher Wren was chosen to be its designer.

The building of the cathedral was to have problems rooted in the dispute between the Church of England and Rome. Those responsible for paying for the new cathedral, the Royal Commission, wanted something Gothic with its connections with the Middle Ages. Wren saw the Gothic style as less civilised and wanted to build something of a more classical design with a huge dome. The classical style, of course, had Italian connections and therefore was seen as papist. The dispute led to a series of delays and the building did not begin until 1675. More delays were caused by the ships carrying the stone for the building, which travelled along the English Channel, being often captured by the French who were once again at war with England from 1688 to 1697 in the War of the Grand Alliance.

The religious bigotry had not ended at the restoration as the dispute over the new St Paul's showed, and it was also evident in other constructions. When the monument to the Great Fire of London was built, there were messages written on each side of it. In 1681 on the West Side of the erection it was written that it was in, 'Sad remembrance of the burning of a Protestant city by the treachery and malice of the Popish faction during a Popish plot.' It seems that any event could be turned to good use to denigrate the Catholic faith without any need for honesty

The Chelsea Hospital was supposedly the idea of Nell Gywnne, the mistress of Charles II.

or proof. The writing was removed during the reign of James II but put back again during the reign of William and Mary. It was not finally removed until 1831.

The building of another famous London monument was begun at this time. The foundation of the Chelsea Hospital was supposedly due to Nell Gywnne after she was approached by a begging soldier. She asked the king to open a home for merited old soldiers. It was begun by Charles, carried on by James and completed by William and Mary who were also responsible for the Naval Hospital at Greenwich. The hospital at Chelsea was occupied by ex-soldiers with no wives or children and who could no longer work. The first pensioner to die in the Chelsea hospital was Simon Box in 1692. He had served under Charles I, Charles II, James II and William and Mary.

Despite the coming of what would seem like civilised society by this time, there was still an air of underlying savagery in London. The fact that personal arguments could be settled in the city using violence was evident when in December 1670 Colonel Blood attacked the Duke of Ormonde and, with four men, dragged the duke away from his coach near Clarendon House, which he had been heading for. The duke was taken along Piccadilly towards Tyburn where Blood planned to hang him for what he had done in Ireland when fighting the Catholic rebels. The duke was only saved when a group of his servants arrived and overpowered Blood and his men. Despite his plans for a public lynching, Blood was pardoned by the king. The fact that someone could do this in public, and then be pardoned by the king, as Blood was, shows what little effect the law had on behaviour. It was still evident that those who were well connected could flout the law.

There was a further example of how some areas of London were seen as outside the law in 1679. This involved pupils from Westminster School. The fact that the school dated from the twelfth century, is one of the original nine public schools in the country and had such eminent pupils as Christopher Wren, John Locke and others would, I believe, have had an influence on the result of the event. A number of the pupils were charged with the murder of a bailiff. It seems that there was a common belief that bailiffs were not allowed to enter the area around the school and when one did go to the home of a local woman, boys from the school rushed to her help, leading to the bailiff's death. The pupils involved were all found not guilty, while the woman who had appealed for their help was found guilty. Obviously she was not as well connected.

The execution of one king had not been enough for some and another plot to kill the present king was hatched in 1683. What became known as the Rye House Plot was planned among forty conspirators, the most senior being the Earl of Essex who eventually killed himself in the tower. The plot was another attempt to stop Catholic sympathies being exercised by the royals. The plan was to kill

Charles II and his brother James who had converted to the Catholic faith. Killing him was the easiest way of stopping his succession as trying to halt this through parliament had already failed.

Grudges were not only settled by men taking their revenge by violence at their own hands. In 1681, Titus Oates used the law to gain revenge on those who he disliked by accusing them of crimes for which they were then punished. It seems that the people Oates accused were denying being part of any popish plot but it was Oates who was believed. It was strange that what Oates was claiming seemed to be believed by so many high-ranking people. Evelyn, in his diary, mentioned meeting Oates and was very suspicious of him from the first meeting. It then seems that Oates even accused the queen of plotting to poison the king. The king himself questioned Oates and it was becoming evident that he was not the man everyone thought he was. Oates had been accused of perjury years before he had come to London, but this does not seem to have been taken into account during his period of popularity. At least fifteen people were executed because of Oates' claims but the king eventually had him thrown into prison. Parliament, however, intervened and released him.

Later, under King James II, Oates was again arrested and thrown into prison. When Oates was later tried it was said that his testimony should not be taken against the life of a dog. He was pilloried and whipped around the streets of London. Even then the story did not end. When William and Mary came to the throne he was again released and given a pension. It seems that Oates had the support of Protestants who believed what he said because it was aimed at Catholics. As with the plaque on the Monument, action against Catholics did not seem to need proof.

The effects of political decisions often resulted in powerful reactions from the people on the streets. In the 1680s Piccadilly was still mainly open land dotted with large mansions. It was also the refuge of numerous footpads and highwaymen, as were most of the western and northern suburbs of London. Incidentally, attacks on travellers on the road by nefarious highwaymen were not all that the population had to fear. In 1681 a group of robbers arrived at Lord Wotton's house on Hampstead Heath on horseback. They then attempted to break down part of the wall to get into the house with the intention of robbing it. Luckily there were a number of people in the house who tried to drive the men off by firing blunderbusses at them. The noise roused the locals and the gang fled.

One of the mansions in Piccadilly was Clarendon House, which was built by Lord Clarendon, the chancellor of Charles II. The house was built after the sale of Dunkirk to the French, an action that angered the mob who thought that the house had been built with money from the French and it became known as Dunkirk House. Clarendon was already unpopular with the public after his daughter married the Duke of York. As the queen had no children, this was seen as a plot by him to gain power. There was even a song made up about Clarendon accusing him of being a traitor. The public then took more direct action to air these views by breaking the windows in his new house.

The death of Charles II in 1685 led to more problems related to religion. Charles had converted to Catholicism on his deathbed and was then succeeded by his brother, James II, Duke of York, himself a Catholic – all of Charles' fourteen children had been illegitimate. The mobs were against the new Catholic king and took to the streets again to destroy Catholic sites that had appeared in the city.

One of the Yeoman Warders – or Beefeaters – of the Tower of London.

Roll Call of the Yeoman Warders at the Tower of London.

There was a fight between the mobs and the army when they tried to burn down St John's Chapel, Clerkenwell.

James did not endear himself to the population when he tried to enforce regard for the Catholic faith and when he ordered the Declaration of Indulgence be read out in churches, many refused to follow his order. Seven bishops were arrested because of this and were taken to the Tower of London, which led to crowds gathering on the streets. When the bishops were found not guilty at their trial, there was rejoicing in the city and the king's days were numbered. In 1688, Mary of Modena, the consort of James II, escaped in a small boat across the Thames to Lambeth. She was followed two days later by James as the Protestant Dutch army of William of Orange marched towards Whitehall, set on ousting the Catholic ruler. As James crossed the Thames he dropped the great seal into the river.

The mobs were out again in 1688 and burnt the Catholic chapel in Lincoln's Inn Fields. They then went on to burn a number of Catholic houses. The reigns of Charles II and James II were marked with mob violence, mainly due to religious intolerance. There was also, strangely, a revival in the popularity of archery during Charles' reign. The mock title of the Duke of Shoreditch first bestowed by Henry VIII was revived and bestowed on the best shot. The archery meetings went on until 1791.

There had been sanctuaries in London in the past but these were mainly religious houses such as the churches. This system was mainly dispensed with in the city but many of the rookeries were occupied by those who lived by theft and begging. As those in authority rarely entered these areas, some saw them as sanctuaries which were not covered by the same rules as the rest of the city and did not come under official jurisdiction. One of these was Whitefriars, which also became known as Alsatia. In July 1691 there was a large fight between the Templars and the Alsatian inhabitants of Whitefriars. The gate between the Temple and Whitefriars had been bricked up to keep them apart but the barrier was pulled down. Two men were killed during the conflict and Captain Francis White, the leader of the Alsatian group, was found guilty of murder.

In 1700 the majority of the population of London lived on the north bank of the Thames. The only built-up area south of the river was Southwark, around London Bridge, which was at this time still the only bridge in London. The small hamlet of Stockwell played a large part in London life at this time. Much larger than its size would suggest, it was the main depot of the smugglers from the south coast who would store their goods in the hamlet and carry them across the Thames on the Horse Ferry at Lambeth. At the time, smuggled goods were purchased by many of those in the highest strata of society, despite the attempts by the government to put an end to the trade.

The streets of the city were not only dangerous with the thieves and highwaymen that occupied its fringes. Gangs of young hooligans roamed the streets throughout the city's history and were known by different names at different times; each often had their own method of behaviour which was not unlike many of the troublemakers of the much more recent past. These gangs were known at various times as Muns, Hectors, Scourers, Nickers, Hawkabites, and Mohocks. Some often used their swords to terrorise the law-abiding population. Robbery in broad daylight was common and the assault of innocent members of the public, including women, was widespread. Not all of these gangs were from the poorer groups of the city either; the Mohocks were famously made up of young men from good families. The only men who were around to stop these mobs were the watchmen or 'Charlies' due to their formation in the reign of Charles, who were often chosen from poor and old people who could not work due to their weakness. They were armed with a pole and one of the favourite pastimes of the gangs of young men who roamed the streets looking for trouble was to turn over the sentry boxes that the watchmen occupied.

Hackney was a very dangerous place in the eighteenth century. There was no chance of the watchmen being any good in keeping order there and Hackney was patrolled by soldiers with guns and bayonets. Hackney Wick was a popular haunt of highwaymen. There was also another military presence in the area as Baumes House at Hoxton was used by the artillery company for gunnery practice. The Baumes March became a favourite exercise for the company.

The reaction by the authorities towards these crimes was to increase the number of capital offences, hoping that this would deter the criminals. This often had the reverse effect, in that, if a man could be hanged for robbery he may as well make sure there were no witnesses and kill his victim. Being hanged for a murder was no different from being hanged for stealing some small item.

Widespread crime did not seem to be enough to bring the population out on the streets but religion still did. In 1710 a clergyman, Henry Sacheverell, attacked

Whigs and Catholics in a sermon which was directed against those who did not follow recognised religion. Sermons obviously had a great deal of influence at this time and he was charged with libel. He was accompanied to his trial by a crowd of around 400 supporters at Westminster Hall. Although he had said that non-resistance to royalty was acceptable, he was accused of using this as a code for resistance. The crowds supporting him got bigger every day that the trial continued and they began to attack meeting houses where other religions met.

Crimes of violence were not only committed by the native population. Robert Harley, Earl of Oxford, was stabbed by a French nobleman, the Marquis de Guiscard, in 1711. Guiscard was then brought before a cabinet council charged with treacherous correspondence with the French Court at St Germain while receiving a pension from England.

In 1714 there was a large military encampment in Hyde Park. Its presence reportedly drew in many women of quality, attracted by the soldiers. The officers at the camp were responsible for giving a number of military balls, which seemed to be the norm relating to military camps. The presence of the camp also had another unexpected result. It made the incidents of theft by footpads in the Kensington area less frequent. The level of crime soon reverted to its old ways once the camp went until armed troopers began to patrol the road to Kensington every night.

There was a problem with highwaymen who were, in many cases, very popular with the public. Those they robbed were usually the better off who travelled on the roads in their coaches and were seen as being rich enough to be able to afford being robbed. Highwaymen often led the procession of condemned criminals from Newgate to Tyburn on execution day. The carts carried the prisoner and his coffin with lesser criminals following the highwaymen. Traitors were at the rear and did not even merit a cart but were pulled on a hurdle. All large gatherings had the potential danger of violence erupting and executions were no different. There were occasions when the victim's body would be taken by surgeons for dissection. This often led to a fight between the victim's family and those sent to collect the body. Along with the violence went crowds of pickpockets. An execution often led to the arrest of numerous criminals who were then executed themselves. The supposed deterrent, then, was actually leading to more crime!

The public place of execution in London was at Tyburn although not all executions were held there. Tyburn was at the corner of Edgware Road. Executions were very public affairs. Highwaymen, seen as public heroes, often went to the gallows gaily and were usually applauded not only by the mob but also by gentlemen and ladies as well. One of the most famous of these was Claude Duval. After 1783 however executions were transferred to Newgate.

Although the problems between Catholics and Protestants may have evolved into an uneasy peace at this time, they were to re-emerge later. Yet another dispute led to trouble on the city's streets, although this time it was between the Jacobites and the Hanoverians. There were opposing public houses in London where supporters of each side would drink and on 10 June 1715, on the birthday of the Old Pretender James Edward Stuart, the crowd from one public house went into the street and forced passers by to drink to his health. This led to a large fight in Drury Lane; these incidents became known as the Mug-House Riots. There would often be attacks on public houses used by one group by those from other public houses favoured by the rivals. The level of violence increased until muskets began to be used to protect public houses from attacks and this inevitably led to deaths. There were then executions of those involved which seemed to settle things down for a time – perhaps the only time that capital punishment did have an effect.

The measures taken by the authorities to deal with disturbances on the streets were not clearly set out. Before any action could be taken against a violent mob, the riot act had to be read. This could only be done when more than twelve people were gathered together and had to be carried out by a magistrate. Magistrates, after reading the act, could then call on constables, yeomanry, militia or troops to deal with the violence. The problem with this system was that some magistrates could be in agreement with the aims of the violent group as came to be seen in later disturbances.

Parts of London were still used for executions of those who committed their crimes outside the city as well as home-grown criminals. Wapping was the place where pirates were executed. Execution Dock was used from as early as the reign of Henry VI but was still being used up until 1735. The bodies of men guilty

The Mug-House Riots were related to the dispute between supporters of the new rulers of the country and the Old Pretender.

An Horizontal View of the PUBLIC FIREWORKS ordered to be exhibited on occasion of the GENERAL PEACE concluded at Aix le Chapelle on November 7th 1748.

A public firework display was held in Green Park to celebrate the end of the war of the Austrian Succession in 1748.

of killing revenue officers were hanged by the river until 1816 as a warning to seamen sailing up the Thames.

The eighteenth century was an incredible time for demonstrations on the streets of the city for some trivial reasons. There was a riot because of a bad play at Covent Garden in 1738, and another due to increased ticket prices at the theatre. Trade disputes were also common with the Thames watermen protesting against new bridges being built and the weavers protesting against imports of cheap calico and against cheap Irish labourers. This became almost a rebellion with 8,000 of them marching on parliament. They then attacked the Duke of Bedford's house because he wouldn't support a duty on imported silk which resulted in troops being stationed throughout London.

Another serious dispute involved the coal heavers who were trying to get more money and more regular work. Then the employers tried to employ blackleg labour which led to some very violent confrontations and which ended in deaths. This continued until once again the troops were called in and the ringleaders of the violence were executed.

❖ ❖ ❖

There were several areas in London which became centres of entertainment. The gardens and bowling green at Marylebone became a popular place for the entertainment of the rich in the mid-eighteenth century and a number of concerts were held there. Getting to Marylebone and home again was, however, a risky business due to the footpads who occupied the area. It was so risky in fact, that guests were normally accompanied both to the gardens and home again by soldiers!

There was a novel form of robbery carried out in St George's Fields in 1754. A group of men posed as a press-gang and preyed on visitors to London. They would grab someone but then offer to release him for the money he was carrying. This must have been a successful method of obtaining money until one man was seized by a real press-gang after being accosted by the false one. The man informed the press-gang of what had occurred and where this had happened and they went and arrested the group of charlatans.

During the early reign of George III, a bill was introduced into parliament that watchmen should sleep during the day to make them more alert during the night. They were only on duty at night despite much of the crime in London being carried out during the day. Mr Nugent MP asked if he could be included in the bill as he had trouble sleeping due to gout.

George III was not a popular monarch on the occasion of his accession. In 1769 a hearse was driven into the courtyard at St James's Palace followed by an angry mob. They were accompanied by Lord Mountnorris, an Irishman who impersonated an executioner.

There was also a serious dispute over the rights of free speech when John Wilkes attacked the king's speech, which led to his imprisonment. This sparked serious riots on the streets and at one point around 40,000 people gathered around the King's Bench prison. The actual election of Wilkes in 1768 had in itself began a riot. It was a custom for the London mobs to meet the Brentford mobs at Knightsbridge. When Wilkes supporters passed, the fighting began.

There seemed to be a more lenient attitude towards religious freedom by the late 1770s and there was an attempt to bring in a Catholic Relief Bill in 1778. This was only short-lived, as suspicions of Catholic plots came to the fore again. This preceded what became known as the Gordon Riots. George Gordon was the sixth child of the Duke of Gordon and a member of parliament. He was responsible for forming the Protestant Association. There was an open-air rally of the association on 2 June 1780 at St George's Fields, an area between Lambeth Palace and the later site of Waterloo station. An estimated 60,000 people came to the rally to protest at the Catholic Relief Bill and later marched to parliament. Many of the lords entering the house were attacked and the commons were trapped inside the house by the mob and had to be freed by soldiers. Then the mob attempted to burn Catholic churches in London. This was not enough for them and they then turned on the homes of Catholics and the large Irish population in Moorfields. The Gordon Riots had begun!

One of the better class areas that suffered from the violence was Bloomsbury. On 7 June, Lord Mansfield's house in Bloomsbury Square was attacked by the mob. The lord just escaped the mob by fleeing through the back door. Mansfield then went to his mansion on Hampstead Heath but was followed by the rioters. The landlord of the Spanish Tavern on the Heath opened his doors to the mob, detaining them with free ale. While they were drinking, the landlord sent for the Horse Guards who arrived and stopped the mob from continuing to Mansfield's mansion.

Meanwhile, Great Russell Street was alight with fires of burning furniture, thrown into the road from the houses of the victims and then torched. Although soldiers did eventually arrive, they were so outnumbered by the crowd that they were powerless to act.

The riots went on for days, mainly due to a lack of action from magistrates and the mayor. As the law stood, the soldiers had to be called out and then allowed to act by the magistrates reading the riot act. Any soldier acting without this permission could be tried for murder. Often soldiers were turned out and then stood by, helpless to intervene as no magistrate would give the order. At one point Lord Erskine stopped the mob at the Temple using the sight of cannon to bring them to their senses. Whether he had a magistrate's permission to do this is unclear.

It seemed as if none of the magistrates or the mayor wanted to be seen helping Catholics owing to the widespread support that the rioters had. When some of the rioters were arrested and imprisoned, the mob attacked the prisons and released them as well as all the other prisoners.

Finally things went too far. Action had to be taken and the army moved in. Gordon now offered to help the army, realising that things had gone too far and were out of control. Hundreds died as the army fought to regain control of the city – the conflict must have been one of the bloodiest disputes to take place in the capital. Many of the victims' bodies were supposedly thrown into the Thames. The more extreme rioters were pursued into the poorest areas of the city. They believed that these areas were immune to action from the authorities. Those who did pursue the rioters were shocked at what they found as most decent people had never been into these rookeries. They were shocked at the poverty and the maze of houses and alleys with so many entrances that escape was easy. The situation in these areas did not change for some time. Henry Mayhew and Charles Dickens told of similar scenes in the mid-nineteenth century.

There were then rumours of French and American involvement in the troubles and after the riots, troops were based on the streets at all times. There was a large army camp in Hyde Park which led to rumours that martial law would be enforced. This in turn led to a dispute between the powers of civil and royal rights. St James's Park was also occupied by regiments of militia because of the riots.

There were reportedly over three hundred people killed and many more wounded by the thousands of troops who were sent onto the streets. Twenty-one rioters were eventually hanged and thousands of pounds were paid to Catholics in compensation. Gordon himself was charged with making war on the king. Gordon's defence was conducted by Thomas Erskine who argued successfully that Gordon did not foresee or have any control over those rioting. Surprisingly, after being found not guilty of causing the riots, Gordon then spent the last five years of his life in Newgate for libel against the British government and Marie Antoinette.

8

THE FRENCH AND NAPOLEON

The slightest trivial incident seemed liable to start a riot in London in the eighteenth century. In 1784 a Frenchman named de Moret attempted to give a display of hot air ballooning, which he charged people to watch, in the rural area west of the city. The balloon had a type of wheeled shed attached to it. Unfortunately the balloon caught fire and did not fly. Instead of showing sympathy, the watching crowd began to riot and destroy local property.

The unpopularity of George III also applied to his son. The future George IV was terribly in debt when he married Caroline of Brunswick. There was a scandal as he had already married in secret to a Mrs Fitzherbert. To make matters worse, Mrs Fitzherbert was a Roman Catholic and so the marriage could not be recognised leaving him able to marry Princess Caroline. Unfortunately, neither George nor Caroline liked each other and the marriage descended into a farce with both of them taking lovers. Despite what was seen by many close to the future king as behaviour not in keeping with that of a princess, Caroline became very popular with the public at large, no doubt partly due to George's own unpopularity. It was the hatred of him that drove people to support his wife.

The end of the century saw the war with France continuing, and by this time thousands of men had volunteered for the various forces to fight them. The area of Somerstown near Euston Road became a popular area for French émigrés escaping the terror of the revolution by fleeing to England. This was also a reason for the Catholic Church of St Aloysius being in Clarendon Square. The French Revolution, although it led to war against France, also opened up a worry that the people of Britain might be influenced by the radical policies of the French and follow their lead. When parliament opened in 1795 there were calls of no war. The government then increased its powers to deal with radicals with acts against treasonable and seditious actions. There was a ban on seditious

William Pitt's statue in Parliament Square. Pitt was prime minister through much of the French Wars of the late eighteenth and early nineteenth century.

meetings and the London Corresponding Society was banned. The fear of the population of London was as serious as the fear of French invasion for many at this time.

The defence of London in case of a French invasion was uppermost in the minds of many people, however. In 1797 an old soldier writing in *The Times* called for an association for the defence of London. This would be organised by provincial gentlemen from each parish who would organise as many of their servants as possible into volunteer groups. The officers of these groups would supply their own horses. Privates who could provide a horse could join the cavalry and every man would supply his own weapon. Although the idea of the formation of a group of men to defend London, which was to evolve into the militia, was a good plan, there were also more unlikely suggestions as to how to defend the capital. In April 1798, again written in *The Times*, a man suggested that blockhouses be built in all London squares along with artillery parks. All corners houses were to be supplied with hand grenades and barricades built at the end of every street. How this would affect the travel through the capital was not mentioned. The writer also called for all obnoxious foreigners (by whom he probably meant all foreigners) to be expelled from the country.

The capital continued to see a large influx of French émigrés who were fleeing the persecutions of the revolution. These people were often brought across the Channel by smugglers, as long as they could pay their way. The French Wars of the late eighteenth and early nineteenth centuries were a problem for London. If the French did choose to invade the country then they would land somewhere in the South-East and, subsequently, would only be a few days' march away from London.

The danger of invasion did not, however, stop the population from expressing their displeasure at some developments. In September 1800 a number of bills were posted on the Monument saying that bread would soon be sixpence a quarter. Following this, a mob attacked a cheese shop in Cheswell Street. Although this was outside the jurisdiction of the city, the mayor decided to attend the incident. A squad of light horse volunteers also arrived and drove the crowd off. The mayor then issued a handbill stating that all peaceable citizens should stay in their homes during events such as this and make sure that their servants did the same. They should also keep away from the windows on the appearance of the military. It seems that the mayor and magistrates had no problem dealing with violence on the streets when the culprits were the lower classes. The following day the mob assembled again in the same area but this time they were driven off by the military. The soldiers stood guard with fixed bayonets but the mob approached Finsbury Square, smashing the lamps as they went.

The fear of invasion had an effect on the highest echelons of society, too. The king, writing from Windsor Castle in 1803 to the Bishop of Worcester, said that he was planning to send his wife and daughters to Worcester in the event of an invasion. While his family went to safety, however, he was hoping to lead the army against the French himself.

To stop important supplies of ammunition falling into the hands of the invasion force, plans were in place to move the contents of the Woolwich Arsenal and the gunpowder magazines at Purfleet to the Midlands by canal. Defending London itself with large defences was not really an option so those built out in Essex were planned to stop an invading army marching on the capital. The danger from a French invasion was that Napoleon, when invading a country, seemed to head for its capital as a matter of course. By taking control of London he would be in complete control of the country's economy. There were plans for a defensive line around the capital in the Duke of York's defence report of 1803. This meant taking in the River Lea. Plans to flood the Lea Valley had been put in place by the engineer John Rennie (who had built London Bridge) and there were sluices erected that would allow the area to flood. Rennie then went off to oversee the Military Canal being built in Kent and Sussex. The defence ring also took in the area around to the high ground of Highgate and Hampstead to the north, round to the Paddington Canal and down to the Norwood Hills in the south and back toward Deptford. There was to be a defensive position built at Shooter's Hill. Much of the ground that this defensive ring took in was still, at that time, open countryside with some remote villages such as Hampstead and Norwood. There was no possibility of building a defensive barrier around this whole perimeter of London, but then the restricted number of any invasion force would make attacks at all points impossible. Therefore the plan was to quickly throw up earthworks at points which looked to be in the line of attack by the enemy. There was another suggestion by a writer to *The Times* in April 1804, that all the church towers in the capital be converted into Martello Towers.

The Duke of York memorial in the Mall. The duke was commander-in-chief of the army during the Napoleonic Wars.

As well as planning the defences of London, the Duke of York also found time to found the Royal Military Asylum behind the Chelsea Hospital. It was to support and educate the children of soldiers, either orphans or those whose fathers had been killed in action. It also admitted children of men on active service whose wives had died. There were 700 boys and 300 girls. The boys would receive military training and the school later became the Duke of York's School.

The Duke of York was a zealous military enthusiast and arranged a number of experiments involving attack and defence by infantry, cavalry and artillery to be carried out in Hyde Park in 1802. This was followed by further experiments on the island of Jersey in 1805 and led to a book on military tactics by Lieutenant John Russell of the 96th Regiment.

There was also another danger from a French invasion and that was the population of the capital itself. A large part of the population, maybe as much as a tenth, were seen as supporting themselves by criminal occupations. This meant that a number of volunteer units, supposedly to be used in defence of the capital, would have to be kept in place to deter any organised uprisings by this underclass.

The end of the Napoleonic Wars led to widespread poverty, which often resulted in protest and machine-breaking by the poor. Some could see that the problems were due to the poverty that many of the lower classes had to endure.

The war was leading to some food shortages and even some of the upper classes decided to help this by refraining from eating certain items. In the Grosvenor Square home of Mr Beckford of Fonthill Abbey, Wiltshire, no bread was taken at dinner due to the wheat shortage. One prominent visitor to the house did not agree with this self-imposed restraint. When Admiral Nelson came to dinner he sent his man out to buy some bread and said that, as he fought for his bread, he thought it hard that his countrymen should deny him it.

On 26 October 1803 the volunteers were paraded in Hyde Park. More than 12,000 Loyal London Volunteers were inspected by the king, the Duke of York, who was commander-in-chief of the army, and four of the king's other sons. On 28 October another 14,000 volunteers from Southwark, Westminster and Lambeth also paraded in the park. There were familiar problems in arming the volunteers as there have been in every conflict. By the nineteenth century, volunteers did not want to be armed with pikes, which there seemed to be plenty of. The thought of mainly untrained volunteers attacking seasoned, well-armed French soldier with pikes is a horrifying thought. The Tower of London became an assembly line for musket parts made elsewhere.

The period also saw the state funeral of one of the heroes of the wars against the French. There were around 8,000 soldiers in the procession at Nelson's funeral after he died at Trafalgar. His body had been carried back to England and sailed up the Thames where it rested at the Naval Hospital at Greenwich. It was later brought into London by barge.

Crowds still gathered in London for other reasons aside from paying their respect to war heroes. Riots on the streets of the city did not stop just because there was a war on. Francis Burdett was to be the last political prisoner in the Tower of London in 1810 and his internment spurred the mobs on to take to the streets again. Burdett had written a letter, which was published in William Cobbett's *Review*. The letter denied the right of parliament to send people to prison and was related to the case of John Gale Jones who had been committed to Newgate for a breach of privilege of the house. Burdett's letter was seen as libellous so the very thing that he had been complaining about then happened to him. The guards were called out and were stood ready to arrest him in Piccadilly although it was actually four days later that constables and soldiers broke into his house and arrested him. The mobs then took to the streets to try to stop him being taken to the tower.

Despite the war that had been going on for some years by this time, the idea of large numbers of soldiers gathered together in barracks was still not popular with some people. This was partly due to the expense. In April 1812 the plans to build new barracks for the Life Guards to replace those in King Street were discussed in parliament. The chancellor of the exchequer said that it was cheaper to build permanent rather than temporary barracks. It was argued why it was now necessary to build barracks where men and horses could be accommodated together, when they had been housed apart for so long? Another reason given for the argument against barracks was that it was said that it was unconstitutional to separate soldiers from the citizens. No doubt the next comment was in response to the situation in the country at the time. It was argued that looms were rendered

The Foot Guards at drill at St John's Wood barracks.

useless while cries of hunger were stifled at the point of the bayonet. The troops who were used to control the population in times of unrest had to be used in areas that they did not come from. Consequently, they had to billeted somewhere when they were moved to other areas.

The war was also to be the period that saw the only assassination of a British prime minister. On 11 May 1812, Spencer Perceval was shot dead in the foyer of the House of Commons to the great shock of everyone in the country. His assassin was a man named John Bellingham who had a colourful past. He had been imprisoned in Russia for debt and had returned to England and tried to claim compensation for his imprisonment which he blamed on the British ambassador to Russia. After shooting the prime minister, he sat on a bench and waited to be arrested, making no attempt to escape. He was sentenced to death and hanged. There must have been some concern over trouble during Bellingham's trial as a report in *The Times* stated that the 1st Regiment of Horse Artillery marched from Knightsbridge barracks on 15 May and were stationed on the Surrey side of Blackfriars Bridge. There was also a detachment of 250 men of the 1st Regiment of Foot stationed in the riding school in Brunswick Street. The military were also called out a few days later when Bellingham was executed.

With the war against France finally over in 1814, or so it seemed at the time, the allied sovereigns who had fought Napoleon gathered in London to celebrate their victory. The group included Emperor Alexander of Russia, the King of Prussia and the King of Belgium. They reviewed the Scots Greys in Hyde Park and the Prince Regent could not keep up with them as they walked because he was so fat. The celebrations over Napoleon's defeat were, of course, premature.

By the nineteenth century, the stock market was an important establishment in London. The war with the French had a big influence on the price of shares; it was said that funds went down every time Napoleon got on his horse. Napoleon was the subject of an event relating to the stock market in February 1815 of a rather sinister nature. A person calling himself Colonel De Bourg, claiming to be an aide-de-camp to Lord Cathcart, arrived at the Ship Hotel in Dover. He claimed that he had come from Paris where Napoleon had been recently been killed by Cossacks and that the llies were marching on Paris and peace was certain. None of this, however, turned out to be true and it seems that at least six persons had made a great deal of money from the hoax by buying and selling shares which rose in value due to the news. Perhaps the best known of these was Lord Cochrane, naval captain and MP for Westminster. It was claimed that not only had he made money from the hoax but that the man claiming to be Colonel De Bourg had gone to his home in London. He was, as a result, expelled from parliament and from the navy. He was also sentenced to a year in prison but believed that he was immune to this punishment as he was an MP. He was, however, eventually arrested in parliament and taken to prison. In March the Committee of the Stock Exchange offered a reward of 250 guineas for the discovery of the person who had instigated the hoax.

There was another story, related by Thornbury, about how money was made on the stock market due to news of Napoleon, but this time it turned out to be based on fact. A Mr F who was the owner of a large estate in Middlesex had lost a fortune on the stock exchange. He was contemplating suicide over his loss when a French ensign informed him that the French ambassador had just told him about the British victory at Waterloo. Mr F supposedly went to a number of firms and told them in confidence of the victory which was not as yet widely known. This allowed them to buy up stocks and shares cheaply, which then went up when the news of victory at Waterloo became public. Mr F was given a share of the profits and had his fortune restored.

The forthcoming battle at Waterloo had aroused great interest in London among soldiers as well as speculators on the markets. The difference in the way the army was organised during this period was shown by the actions of an officer named Rees Howell Gronow. Despite being on duty at St James's, he sent his two horses and groom abroad to Ostend and followed himself, despite not having any leave. He hoped to be able to be at the battle and then get back in time to be on guard at St James's.

The victory at Waterloo was announced to the rulers of the country at the home of a Mrs Boehm in St James's Square on 21 June 1815. The Prince Regent, Castlereagh and other politicians were dining at the lady's house. Shouting and the noise of a coach being followed by crowds attracted the attention of others in the area before it arrived at Mrs Boehm's home. Lady Bronlow, who also lived in the square, saw the coach, which had French eagles sticking out of the windows, stop at Castlereagh's house (he also lived in St James's Square). The coach then went on to Mrs Boehm's house after finding that Castlereagh was not at home. It was carrying

A SILLY TRICK.

JOHN BULL.—"COME, COME, YOU FOOLISH FELLOW; YOU DON'T SUPPOSE I'M TO BE FRIGHTENED BY SUCH A TURNIP AS THAT!"

The nineteenth century saw numerous scares of invasion by the French. Not all of them were taken seriously by everyone.

Major Henry Percy who had arrived from the Duke of Wellington with news of victory at Waterloo. The prince supposedly cried, despite the victory, for the many friends that he had lost in the battle. The victory at Waterloo was celebrated in Hyde Park with a mock naval engagement taking place on the Serpentine.

Despite the continuing dispute over the building of barracks, they were still appearing in London at the time of the French Wars. Wellington Barracks in Bird Cage Walk opened in 1814 for the household troops. Since the formation of the guards in the time of Charles II, they had had no barracks. The guards had been stationed around Whitehall and received higher pay than other members of the army. The armoury which had stood in Bird Cage Walk was the origin of the guards' barracks. The Riding House in Hyde Park had been used as headquarters for the Westminster Volunteer Cavalry. It was later used to stage a Waterloo exhibition.

In 1816 the Spa Fields Riots took place. There were an enormous number of people, up to 20,000, at the meeting. They were led by a man named Watson. There were supposed to be plans for the mob to take the Tower of London and the Bank of England and the leaders were arrested. It seems, however, that the information had come from a government spy whose word was suspect and although the leaders were arrested they were later released.

The end of the war did not keep the mobs happy for long. There were riots in the West End in 1816 upon the establishment of the Corn Laws. In *Recollections and Reflections* by Mr Planche, he remembered seeing artillerymen drawn up with loaded field pieces and lighted matches in Berkeley Square during the days of Lord Liverpool's ministry.

The home of the Earl of Harrowby was at 29 Grosvenor Square and was the planned site of one of the most daring political assassination attempts in British political history. The cabinet of George IV were dining there on 23 February 1820. A gang of twelve men, led by Arthur Thistlewood, planned to take action against the politicians. Thistlewood was an ex-soldier who had already served twelve months in prison for annoying Lord Sidmouth and challenging him to a duel when he failed to respond to Thistlewood's correspondence. He had also been present at the Spa Fields Riots and had been involved in a number of earlier plots and uprisings since the beginning of the century.

The men met in a stable loft in Cato Street and the episode became known as the Cato Street Conspiracy. The building was a three-stall stable that had been taken over by a man named Harris a month earlier. The plan was that one of the men would deliver a false despatch to the house where the cabinet were meeting and, when the door was opened, the rest would rush in and kill all the politicians present. They would then go to Hyde Park Barracks where they hoped to attract help from the soldiers. They would then attack the Bank of England and the Tower of London. When the plot was discovered (Lord Harrowby had been informed of it while riding in Hyde Park), the dinner was changed to Lord

The room above a stable in Cato Street where one of the most daring attempts at taking over control of the government was hatched.

Liverpool's home – although the preparations for the meal at Harrowby's had to be continued in case the plotters were watching the house. A plan to trap the men was made by the Duke of Wellington but this involved the cabinet carrying on with their planned meeting which was seen as being too dangerous. It was a grand plan that never had the opportunity to be put into practice. It seems that rumours of the plot were rife at the time.

The men were surprised by Bow Street Runners in the stable. Nine of them were caught and sent to the Tower of London and the leader, Thistlewood, and three others were sentenced to death. The others were all transported. It seems that the men were so sure that their actions would be supported by the population that they planned to parade through the streets with the heads of their victims on poles.

Despite the plots and troubles on the streets at this time, there were still those who argued against barracks being built for soldiers. The arguments against were raised again in June 1820 when Mr Bennet MP said in the house that the evils resulting from soldiers constantly associating together in large bodies were known to everyone. Was it safe to have them under one roof with arms, which could be used for civil mischief? He also stated that there was already such a multitude of barracks in London was it necessary or worth the risk of having more?

Another source of conflict after the war was the treatment of the queen. Sir Matthew Wood had been the Lord Mayor in 1816–17 and he supported Queen Caroline in the disputes between her and her husband. Even during the coronation of George IV in January 1820, the queen was insulted by being refused entry to Westminster Abbey during the ceremony. The support for Queen Caroline was in many ways a reaction to the unpopularity of her husband. Even as a prince, he had not been popular – not only with the public but also with his father who refused to give him a military command despite his brother being commander-in-chief of the army. Instead, the prince had to be happy with wearing elaborate uniforms which meant nothing. The situation came to a head at the queen's funeral in August 1821, at which there was serious violence. The funeral of Queen Caroline was an obvious target for trouble after the way she had been treated by George IV. The plan was to remove her body from Brandenburg House, where she had died, and take it to Harwich where it could be sent back to her homeland. Although a military guard was planned for the coffin, the authorities did not want it to travel through London as they suspected that this would cause problems. The result was that the planned route itself caused offence to many people. A large crowd turned out on the day the procession began and blocked the route planned for the coffin, with carts forcing it to go through the city. When trouble did begin it was at the gates of Hyde Park where huge crowds had gathered to watch the queen's body pass. The troops on duty were trying to force open the park gates that had been shut. They were then pelted with stones by the mob. When the troops opened fire they were acting without permission of a magistrate and were therefore responsible for the murder of two men who died.

❖ ❖ ❖

The final passing of the Catholic Emancipation Bill occurred in 1828. Although it may have seemed that the time was eventually right for this, there was still ill feeling against Catholics. The Duke of Wellington, who was prime minister at the time, lost popularity with the public over the matter of the bill, despite his previous respect as one of the country's leading soldiers. His home,

The Duke of Wellington was to become one of England's best-known and most successful soldiers. He was also later to become a politician and a familiar figure in London.

Apsley House, formerly known as number one London, home of the Duke of Wellington and now the Wellington Museum.

The statue of Wellington, which stands opposite Apsley House at Hyde Park Corner.

The statue of Achilles in Hyde Park was cast from French cannon captured during the Napoleonic Wars and is a tribute to Wellington.

Apsley House in Hyde Park, was attacked and the windows were smashed which led to him fitting metal blinds over all the windows. On another occasion he was abused by a mob while on his way home from the Tower of London. Wellington's popularity was only restored after he fought a duel with the Earl of Winchilsea.

Apsley had a military history as the site was supposedly given to a soldier by George II. The man named Allen had fought with the king at the Battle of Dettingen. The house itself was given to Wellington in 1820 on a lease; he then bought it in 1830. Behind the house in Hyde Park is the statue of Achilles, which was raised in his honour by the ladies of England. It was cast from captured French cannon and designed by Sir Richard Westmacott in 1822. It was criticised at the time because of its nakedness.

During the Reform Riots of 1830 the situation was so bad that the king, William IV, declined to attend the city festivities. John Key, the Lord Mayor elect, said that if Wellington came to dine with the new Lord Mayor he should be accompanied by a guard. A number of volunteer groups were formed to help calm the situation. This included 400 ward constables, 250 porters, 150 firemen, 130 extra hired men, 300 tradesmen, 150 from the artillery company and 600 East India Company volunteers. Despite this the Horse Guards still had to be called out.

In the previous year, 1829, the need for a recognised police force in the city had been finally addressed. With a proper police force it was hoped that there would be less need for volunteers every time there was a crisis. There had been calls for many years to replace the watchmen system, which was as good as useless. The new police then took to the streets of the capital. This was not without some protest by a number of the population. The newspapers were quick to pick up on any adverse incidents involving the police, such as the following incident in Pimlico in October 1829. The event was described as a disgraceful occurrence when two police officers dragged a respectable gentleman to the watch house. The man turned out to be aged over seventy and had been seriously ill. While walking his dog in company with his son, some men had come out of a public house with a dog which had attacked the elderly gentleman's dog. While trying to stop the attack, the man was approached by two policemen who accused him of being drunk and arrested him. They then threatened to knock down the man's son who tried to explain the situation. It was said that the man might never recover from the incident despite being released as soon as someone spoke up for him and told the police who he was.

Despite negative comments on the new police by the press, a number of people wrote to the newspapers to give their support for the new force. Many believed that the streets of London were much safer and more peaceful since their arrival. There was also a view, however, that the presence of the police had not stopped crime but driven it into other areas.

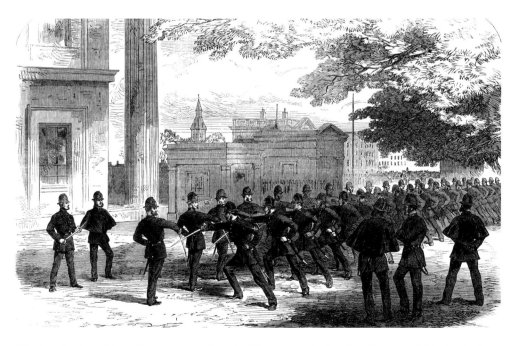

The introduction of the police was not well received by everyone in London. Because of this they had to learn to defend themselves with cutlass training at Wellington Barracks.

The actual duties of the police were, it seems, far from understood by the population of the capital. One man wrote to *The Times* to ask if the police were allowed to stop and search respectable tradesmen. The reply given was that they needed a good reason to do so – an argument that has not been fully settled in the past 180 years.

There were a number of serious disputes in 1830 involving the police. One took place at Temple Bar when a crowd gathered and shouted 'down with the new police!' The crowd were then assaulted by the police and twelve were arrested. In another incident, the king was returning from the theatre in Covent Garden and large crowds gathered. They followed the king to the gates of St James's Park, shouting their disapproval of the police, where they were stopped by the soldiers on duty. The crowd cheered for the Oxford Blues before heading to Leicester Square, continually shouting. There was a violent reaction and four police officers had to take refuge in the Chedray's Hotel after they were attacked. When reinforcements arrived, twenty people were arrested. This included a soldier of the 16th Lancers who was charged with assault on the police. He had supposedly inspired the mob to attack the police officers and claimed that if he had his sword, all the policemen in London would die.

Following a meeting at the Rotunda at Blackfriars against the police and the reform bill, the crowds tried to approach the House of Commons. The police stopped them, which resulted in serious violence. The year of 1830 also saw the first police officer killed on duty; PC Joseph Grantham was killed at Somers Town, Euston. By this time the newspapers seemed to have changed their view of the new force. When a mob of 150 men was reported to have gathered in the Haymarket in November 1830 to confront the police, they were described as mechanics and thieves. How the press came to the conclusion that they were thieves was not clear, but it obviously influenced the readers against the group when the violence between the men and the police was reported.

There was a monster rally on Kennington Common against the reform bill. It was not that the people were against reform but that the bill did not go far enough and grant rights to enough people. Troops were once again based in Hyde Park, the Tower of London and a number of other sites. It seems that by the time of the rally, lessons had been learnt by the authorities. Only those taking the petition were allowed across the river from Kennington to parliament. The rest, thought to number 40,000, were left trapped, knowing that the soldiers would come if there were any attempt to make their way towards the house.

By February 1832 the question of London barracks again came up in parliament but for a different reason this time. Sir H. Hardinge called the attention of the house to the state of the guards. Many of them were in quarters in Bethnal Green and Tothill Fields. Hardinge stated that if cholera broke out in these areas, then when the soldiers appeared on parade they would spread it to the barracks. He said that they should all be moved to houses close to the barracks. His fears seem to have been fully justified as in August that year, new recruits for the guards were stationed at Warley in Essex. They were due to travel up to London but were told to remain at Warley due to an outbreak of cholera at the London barracks.

9

VICTORIAN LONDON

The reign of Queen Victoria is remembered as the period of a number of wars overseas as the British Empire expanded. Usually, home life in London at the time is seen as a prosperous and peaceful period as the industrial revolution made numerous people rich. This may have been true of the middle and upper classes but was far from being the case for the workers who filled the new factories.

There was a serious threat to the queen on a number of occasions. In this incident a pistol was fired at Her Majesty in Hyde Park in May 1840.

The man who fired the pistol was quickly overcome by members of the public.

All was not well as there were actually three attempts on Victoria's life during the 1840s. The first, by a man named Edward Oxford, took place in 1840. Oxford was only nineteen when he made his attempt on the queen's life and he claimed that an army of revolutionaries would rise up at his command. He was obviously insane and was sent to Bethlem Royal Hospital (Bedlam) and then to Broadmoor. He was finally released after twenty-seven years and then left the country.

In 1842 a man named John Francis tried to kill the queen. Francis was sentenced to death but this was later commuted to transportation. There was a further attempt in 1849 when a man named Hamilton also tried to kill her. The attack by Hamilton took place in Hyde Park when the queen was returning from a drive in the park with Prince Albert and some of her children. They had reached Constitution Hill when Hamilton fired a pistol at them from inside the park. Hamilton was arrested by a constable and a park keeper, who had to rescue him from a mob that had gathered round him, and taken to the station house in Gardener's Lane, King Street, Westminster.

Hamilton was an Irish labourer who had obtained the pistol from his landlady in Pimlico on the pretence of cleaning it. He had then bought powder and took the gun to Hyde Park. From a witness statement it seemed that he did not know the

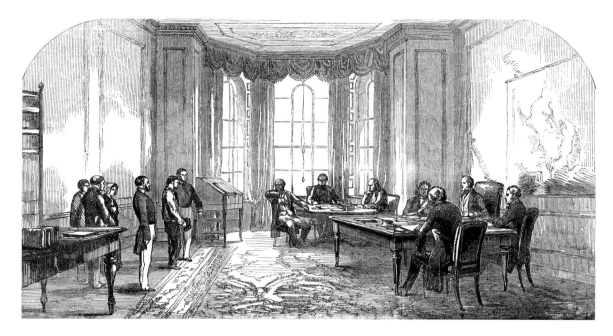

The examination of the prisoner who turned out to be Irish was conducted at the Home Office.

queen was about to pass until a lady told him. From examination of the weapon it seemed that it did not even contain any ball, just powder. It turned out that Hamilton had been unemployed for some time and had committed the act as a demonstration against his poverty. He was committed to Newgate to await trial.

There were in fact eight attempts to either kill the queen or seriously injure her during her reign. Perhaps the strangest was the final attempt by Roderick MacLean in March 1882. He tried to shoot the queen at Windsor because of a curt reply from the royal family to the poetry that he had sent them. At his trial he was found to be insane and sentenced to Broadmoor where he died in 1921. The event was immortalised in a poem by William McGonagall who some claim to have been the worst poet in the English language.

The 1840s was a decade of serious trouble in the city and one famous name did his bit to help out, despite it not being his country. In 1847 Prince Louis Napoleon was in exile in London. He was living in King Street and often rode in Hyde Park. The prince served as a special constable in the fight against the Chartist Risings of 1848. It seems that despite the now-established police force, volunteers were still needed to help keep the peace.

There was a meeting held in Trafalgar Square in March 1848 by mainly working class men protesting against an increase in income tax. There were between 5,000 and 10,000 people in the square when 500 police officers tried to clear the area.

The newspapers reported that the police were overzealous and several respectable people were injured. The press taking the side of the protestors was an unusual event in itself. The police were then beaten back to Scotland Yard. More police arrived and there were running skirmishes throughout London. The police also asked for help from the army but they did not leave their barracks.

The revolutions taking place in Europe were, it seems, having an effect on the population of London. As well as the danger of war owing to the unsettled situations in other countries, some of the ideas of these revolutions were reaching the city. The *Illustrated London News* of 26 May 1849 published an article about the revolutionary literature that was reaching London from Europe. Much of it was French but had been translated into English. The article mentioned the works of Louis Blanc and Proudhon and their revolutionary socialist ideas. It also went on to mention the works of men whose ideas opposed these, such as Lord Brougham, M. Thiers and M. Guizot who had written in defence of capitalism. The article actually gave a well-balanced review of both sides of the argument which was much more open and honest than one would have expected.

Later in the century, a reported 15,000 were present at the funeral of the Duke of Wellington. On 18 November 1852 the body of the duke was carried from the

The death of Wellington led to enormous crowds attending his lying in state. He was buried in St Paul's Cathedral.

Horse Guards, where the control of the British army was held throughout much of the country's history.

Wellington Arch was originally known as Constitution Arch. It originally had a statue of Wellington on top but this was later moved to Aldershot after Wellington's death. Now it has a statue of the angel of peace on the chariot of war.

Chelsea Hospital where it had lain in state along Horse Guards Parade. Tickets were given out to various visitors to pay their respects on various days followed by four days of public opening. The crush was so bad on these days with so many people wanting to see the duke's body that four people died.

There was a strange report in the *Illustrated London News* of 26 August 1854 concerning St John's Wood Barracks. The barracks had been opened on what had been farmland in 1822. They had been cavalry barracks and had also been used as a riding school where a number of men from cavalry regiments would learn to ride by balance. These men would then return to their regiments as instructors. In 1832 the riding school lease had expired but the premises had been taken up again for use as infantry barracks. This was the subject of a number of complaints against the theory that the government was trying to encircle London with troops by positioning them in barracks in the suburbs. The fact that this fear should have been raised in a newspaper while the Crimean War was in progress seems strange

Weapons captured in the Crimean War were exhibited at Crystal Palace.

timing. One would think that the presence of the 150 men of the Grenadier Guards based there would have been a comfort to the population while the war was being fought.

The despatch of troops from London had begun in 1854 when the government decided to send 10,000 troops to Malta. Included in this were the Scots Fusilier Guards. Before leaving, they paraded at Buckingham Palace on 28 February. The queen and the royal family came out onto the balcony to take a salute from the regiment. This was followed by three cheers for the queen from the men.

There were obviously problems in the London barracks during the Crimean War. In January 1855 not only was there serious disease in the Crimea but also in the barracks in London. The hospitals for the Foot Guards were overflowing which was partly due to overcrowding in barracks. The barracks at Charing Cross and St James's Park were overflowing while those at the Tower of London were only half full.

The news of victory in the Crimean War led to scenes of jubilation in London as crowds gathered to celebrate. Under orders from Lord Hardinge, twenty-five

To celebrate the victory in the Crimea, the guns at the Tower of London were fired at six o'clock in the morning.

The guns were also fired at St James's Park no doubt to wake those who could not hear the guns at the tower.

guns were fired in St James's Park at six o'clock in the morning to celebrate, attracting a large crowd. The guns were fired again at twelve. The guns at the Tower of London on the new saluting battery were also fired.

The Crystal Palace exhibition was very military-biased and there were regular concerts by the bands of the Life Guards, Grenadier Guards, Scots Fusilier Guards and the Royal Artillery. The Crimean War having only just finished at the time, some of the exhibits also had a distinctly military flavour. This included the display of a gun and a mortar captured at the Siege of Bomarsund. The weapons were not the only things to arrive from the battle. A number of both Russian and Finnish prisoners from Bomarsund were brought to Britain and held on hulks at Sheerness before being moved to permanent prisons.

The military also had an effect on the finances of the population of London when in 1857 a large army clothing works opened at Pimlico. Before this, numerous contractors had supplied army clothing and many made a fortune out of it. The factory became the largest employer of women in London and kept getting bigger. By 1859 it covered 7 acres and employed more than 1,000 workers. Working conditions were very good for the time, but employment rules were strict. No women with young children (who were likely to affect their attendance) were employed there.

There was a further outbreak of violence in the city in the mid-nineteenth century, which gained much greater publicity than the actual number of events deserved. One of the best-known incidents involved an MP named Pilkington who was robbed between his club and parliament. It was not the person involved or the place that aroused interest but the method of robbery that became publicised. An assailant would loop a rope around the victim's neck and strangle him while an accomplice went through their pockets. The method became known as garrotting and achieved a terrific level of panic that gripped

The nineteenth century saw the foundation of numerous volunteer units of the army, some with elaborate uniforms.

Being photographed in military uniform became a respectable event for middle class volunteers who had none of the bad image of regular soldiers.

the city and was reported in newspapers such as *The Times*. The main suspects, according to the press, were foreigners, as it was not seen as the sort of crime that an Englishman would commit. There were calls for swaggering foreigners such as the Italians in Whitechapel, who carried stilettos, to be deported. Of course many of those who were caught for committing this crime turned out to be English.

In the past there were numerous burial grounds in the city. Many of these were continually over-used, with previously buried bodies being dug up and reburied in large pits or even burned to make space for new burials. Often the old bones from these burial grounds were gathered up and moved elsewhere so that land could be built on. Often bones and even partly decomposed bodies were left a few feet below the surface in many of these old burial grounds. One of these was at the Church of the Holy Redeemer, Clerkenwell, built on the site of the old Spa Fields Chapel. After being closed as a burial ground in 1853 due to overcrowding, it became a drill ground for the 3rd Middlesex Artillery and the 39th Middlesex Rifles. It later became a children's playground.

The War Department was formed in 1856 and had offices in Pall Mall. The secretary of state for war became the controller of the army from this point which took away many of the powers of the commander-in-chief who, it was said, from this point on became a puppet of the government.

The same period saw the foundation of several volunteer military units in response to the fear of the French and their expanding navy. These included such well-known units as the Artists Rifles and were made up of mainly middle class men, as they had to buy their own equipment – something which was beyond the means of the normal working class men. The volunteers were in some ways more

The Artists Rifles were a very upper-class volunteer unit. Their previous headquarters in Duke Street is now a college.

A transport wagon of the 1st Surrey Regiment, based in South London.

acceptable socially than the regular forces. The men could indulge in their passion for wearing uniforms and expressing military virtues without the vices of the real soldier. The army had never had a popular image with soldiers being seen as quite degenerate, especially during periods of peace. The London volunteer units were especially good at recruiting a better class of young man whose background was probably that of a public school.

Another series of riots began in 1862 and were known as the Garibaldi Riots. There was a rally in Hyde Park in September when between 10,000 and 20,000 people turned up to support Garibaldi's attempts to unite Italy. The gathering was then attacked by a mob of Irish supporters of Rome. A number of off-duty Grenadier Guards were only too happy to help in the fight against the Irish who then ran off but attacked again later. By October the Irish had a number of Italian monarchist helpers and there was fighting in other parts of London.

The number of Irish immigrants in London in the middle of the nineteenth century was more than 100,000. This was partly due to the depression in the country after the Napoleonic Wars. Ireland had been an ideal recruiting ground for some professions in those times, such as the Coastal Blockade that was formed to combat smuggling. The number of Irish immigrants was further swollen by the

The Central London Rangers with a lethal-looking weapon.

potato famine of the 1840s. Added to these immigrants were a number of Irish soldiers who at the end of England's wars were discharged onto London's streets. Irish ghettos grew in many areas and were dangerous, filthy and overcrowded places, much like the earlier rookeries that had existed in London for many years.

As the open spaces in the city began to disappear, swallowed up by building projects, places such as Hyde Park was one of the few venues left where crowds could still gather when there was something to demonstrate about. Another venue then beginning to gain popularity as the place to demonstrate, Trafalgar Square, was far from popular with the authorities.

The 1860s also saw the outbreak of Fenian violence in the city. The Irish Republican Brotherhood held its first meeting in London in 1861. Although the movement was Irish-based, it had in fact begun in America. In 1867 there was an attack on three soldiers in Bloomsbury. There followed an attack on Clerkenwell prison by Fenians trying to release one of their members named Burke. The attack led to a large explosion, although there was obviously a lack of experience with explosives displayed by the attackers. The bomb that blew up the prison wall also demolished nearby houses killing six people. Although a large number of the prisoners in the prison escaped, Burke, the actual target of the attempt, did not.

A well attended trade union demonstration in Waterloo Place in February 1867.

The instigators of the explosion were to have a claim to fame for another reason. Michael Barrett, who was found guilty of planting the bomb, was to be the last person executed in public in Britain in May 1868. After this, executions were moved inside Newgate prison.

The court records for the Old Bailey for the 1860s include a number of cases of murder and assault where the reason given for the incident was that the attacker had been called a Fenian by his victim. Several of these defendants were described as wearing Fenian, or billycock, hats. These were similar to bowler hats and were popular with the Fenian movement in Canada.

The media were reporting threats of Fenian attacks on the armouries of the military volunteer units in London in early 1881. The 1st Surrey Rifle Volunteers had their headquarters at Camberwell and were ordered to be on their guard against any attacks by Fenians. The Royal Arsenal was also thought to be in danger of attack and there were explosions and shootings linked to Fenians taking place at other places in the country. At the time, guns could be bought by anyone for as cheaply as a few shillings. Many criminals carried them as a matter of course and it was also common practice for criminals to pawn their guns in lean spells.

There were further Fenian attacks in the 1880s. In 1883 there were attacks on *The Times* offices, Whitehall, Charing Cross, Westminster and Praed Street, where sixty people were injured. The year 1883 was to see the first attack on the London Underground, on a train travelling between Charing Cross and Westminster stations. At first the underground explosions were thought to have been caused by an anarchist group but were in fact due to a Fenian attack.

Although the police had begun to use detectives as early as 1840 to combat the terrorist attacks, the Special Branch was formed in 1883 as another part of the police force. The new department was at first known as the Special Irish Branch. In 1884 there were attacks on Victoria station, Nelson's Column, Scotland Yard, the Tower of London, the Carlton Club, Tower Bridge and Westminster Hall.

The 1880s also saw violence in the city from Fenian groups. This bomb exploded at Great Scotland Yard and was an attack on the police.

There was also a Fenian attack on the Junior Carlton Club in St James's Square.

A boat full of dynamite was also exploded under the second arch from the Surrey side of London Bridge.

There were more attacks in 1885 when three bombs exploded simultaneously at Westminster Hall, the House of Commons and the Tower of London. There were some injuries in these attacks. The power to strike at the centre of London shows just how organised the early Fenian movement was.

Although it would seem that religious persecution was over by the late nineteenth century, a move by the government in 1874 led to more rioting based on religious differences in the city. The Public Worship Regulation Act was a private members' bill introduced by the Archbishop of Canterbury and its aim was to limit ritualism in Church of England services and end Anglo Catholic tendencies in the church. The bill was supported by Queen Victoria and by the prime minister, Benjamin Disraeli, and it became law despite the wishes of many who objected to it.

A number of priests carried on with their normal practices despite the new law. These included Arthur Tooth who was the vicar at St James's Church in Hatcham. Because of Tooth's views, the church was regularly besieged by mobs of Protestants on Sundays and damage was done to the church. When mobs of supporters of Tooth's views also gathered at the church there was violence on a regular basis. Tooth was one of five priests in the country who were imprisoned for practising their beliefs in what was by this time seen as a free country.

A public movement was founded to support the imprisoned clergymen and posters were printed and distributed stating that Victorian persecution was history repeating itself. The posters included a list of martyrs from the earliest days of Christianity up to the imprisoned priests of the present day.

Trouble in London in late Victorian times did not only come from Fenians and those with religious grudges. There had been large gatherings of unemployed men in 1886. There was said to be some excitement at Bow Street police court in February as there was an indication that warrants were to be sworn for the arrest of the organisers of these demonstrations. There were more police on duty in the city and it was this that had led to rumours of further demonstrations being planned.

There had also been numerous claims for damages from those who had suffered due to the recent riots in the West End. Because of this damage, these gatherings had been banned in the streets. For some reason, however, the following Sunday the unemployed again gathered in Trafalgar Square. This should not have been allowed but large numbers of police were ready for trouble at Scotland Yard and three extra companies of Grenadier Guards were based at St George's barracks. Some of the men from Trafalgar Square went to Westminster Abbey and caused problems during a service. There were then several clashes with the police as the men returned to Trafalgar Square after the service at the abbey. Later, to assist the

The late nineteenth century saw a number of violent demonstrations of London's streets. This one was in St James's Street in February 1886.

There was damage to a number of shops in the West End in the February 1886 riots. These shops in Piccadilly were looted by the mob.

As well as mounted soldiers, there were also mounted police who tried to disperse crowds of demonstrators. This incident took place at the Grand Hotel.

police, the Life Guards arrived in the square. The first arrivals were a contingent of 200 troopers commanded by a Colonel Talbot and accompanied by Mr Marsham, a magistrate. Another 150 Life Guards then arrived under Colonel Dundonald. They encircled the square but never approached the mob. Then the Grenadier Guards under Major Creighton arrived with fixed bayonets. Each man also had twenty rounds of ammunition for their rifles. They formed up in front of the National Gallery and drove the crowd back onto the square, out of the roadway. The guards were ordered to put up their weapons but used their rifle

The army were often brought in to help the police during demonstrations. In this incident the Life Guards were used to clear Trafalgar Square.

butts to crush the toes of any demonstrator who got too close. Three hundred of the protestors were arrested and some got six months' hard labour. Around 150 were treated in hospital.

The trouble with the police and army did not lead to an end to demonstrations and meetings. Some meetings took place in Hyde Park during October 1887. These also led to a number of clashes with the police. Eventually, meetings by large numbers of people in Hyde Park were barely tolerated while those held in Trafalgar Square were not accepted at all. This was despite an argument put

Although demonstrations in Hyde Park were often tolerated, the display of a red flag seemed to have been too much of a provocation to the police.

Not all processions in London were made up of demonstrators. Here we see the Guards marching along the Thames Embankment.

forward at Bow Street police court in November 1887 by Mr W.M. Thompson, a barrister, that Lord Coleridge had decided that processional demonstrations were a legitimate use of the streets. He was therefore trying to claim damages against the police for assault while acting under the orders of Sir Charles Warren, the commissioner of police, against demonstrators during a riot the previous week.

While this was going on, the London Radical clubs had decided that a demonstration due for the following weekend would take place in Hyde Park. The more militant members, however, declared that it was their right to meet in Trafalgar Square and meant to seize the opportunity to speak from the plinth of Nelson's Column.

While these arguments raged back and forth, the forces of law and order were gathering their men together. A large number of special constables were also being sworn in at the Guildhall. The volunteers were members of the stock exchange, solicitors, accountants and clerks. Perhaps the type of person one would expect to do so. However, there were also some less expected types of volunteer, including large numbers of porters from the South Eastern Railway. The men were all issued with batons and were subject to sessions of drill.

There were attacks of a more sinister kind in the East End in 1888. A number of prostitutes were horribly murdered by the person who became known as Jack the Ripper. There was some suspicion that the culprit may have been a man known as 'leather apron' who had assaulted some prostitutes in the Whitechapel area. The rumour was that the person was of a foreign extraction. This was reinforced when a witness saw one of the victims speaking to a foreign-looking man just before she was murdered. It was suspected that the murderer may have been Jewish which led to a new wave of anti-Semitic feeling. As with most crimes that filled people with horror, the population refused to believe that they could have been carried out by an Englishman.

The late nineteenth century finally saw attempts to fortify the city against attack as no defences had been built since the Civil War. Building walls around the capital was not a feasible plan so an idea was drawn up by Lieutenant Colonel Ardargh in 1887, who was the deputy director of military intelligence. He had plans for entrenched camps at Epping and Brentwood to stop any force that landed on the east coast approaching London. The final result was a series of planned small redoubts along the North Downs, south of the city, and at Epping and North Weald to the east. In the end, only those at North Weald were actually built.

The final outcome of the defence debate was a plan that said defences would only be built if there were a threat. It was thought that these could be completed within four days and would consist of 400 field guns and thirteen forts around the city. The majority of the defences would have consisted of earthworks and the plan was very similar to what had been put in place during the Civil War.

Recruitment practice for the army had changed by this time, even for officers. To become an officer in the army in the late nineteenth century, applicants had to pass an entry test. One man who was to make his name as a soldier, writer and politician was Winston Churchill – and he failed the entrance exam for Sandhurst twice! To help him get around this he went to a crammer run by a Captain James in the Cromwell Road, London. The view was that anyone who was not an idiot could pass after attending this school. The school based their success on knowing the kind of questions asked in the entrance test. Despite this help, Churchill was only successful in obtaining a pass at the lower end of the scale and was admitted to a cavalry cadetship at Sandhurst. As life in the cavalry was more expensive than the infantry, there was less competition for places.

10

THE TWENTIETH CENTURY

The beginning of the new century saw the rise of violent anarchist activity across Europe, and London was not excluded from this. Some groups arrived here from abroad and carried on with their subversive activities which often included violent robberies to raise the money needed for their causes.

His Majesty King George V has expressed a wish that the Army Pageant should be in no way postponed owing to the recent National calamity.

An Army Pageant was held at Fulham Palace in 1910 in aid of the Soldiers' and Sailors' Help Society, despite the recent national calamity mentioned in the leaflet, which was the death of the new king's father, Edward VII.

Apart from the danger of anarchists there was also a worrying belief that, in the case of a war in Europe, there would not be enough men left to protect the country when the army was sent overseas. Defence against invasion would fall mainly on the shoulders of the Territorial Army and many politicians thought that this would not be good enough and wanted conscription. This was strictly fought against; even when the war began conscription did not begin for some time. The army council believed that the strength of the territorial forces was good enough to repel an invasion force of 70,000. There were still attempts, however, to recruit more men and the City of London Territorials marched through the streets of the city attracting large crowds in an effort to gain more recruits.

The results of incidents in other countries also led to trouble on the streets of London. In October 1909 there was a rally of socialists in Trafalgar Square against the execution in Spain of Francisco Ferrer. The Ferrer Rioters, as they became known, marched from Trafalgar Square to the Spanish Embassy. Along the route they were continually charged by mounted police until they were eventually dispersed. Ferrer had opened schools in Spain where both boys and girls could learn together in a non-church controlled system. In the strongly religious country that Spain still was, this set him against both the church and the state. When Spain had taken over Morocco there had been a wave of strikes and demonstrations against the use of force in the country. In Barcelona the disputes became very violent and led to over 600 deaths among the protestors. Despite not even being in Barcelona at the time, Ferrer was accused of being the leader of the troubles. It seems that the government used the unrest as an excuse to rid themselves of him. After a one-sided trial in which there was very little (if any) evidence against him, he was executed.

In 1910 a miners' strike in Glamorgan led to several violent clashes with the police. In response to this, Winston Churchill sent not only hundreds of Metropolitan Police officers to Glamorgan, but also troops. He was criticised for this but the troops did not have any role in the violence. The same could not be said of the London police, however, who were involved in some of the more violent clashes with miners.

In 1911 there was to one of the best-remembered pre-war events in the East End when two men involved in a robbery were chased by the police and took refuge in a flat at 100 Sidney Street. In the ensuing shoot-out with the armed men, a policeman was killed. As usual, the military were used to help deal with any situation involving violence and the Scots Guards were also on site to help deal with the siege. A well-known personality also turned up to help – Winston

A squad of rifle volunteers in London in what were obviously pre-First World War uniforms.

Churchill – who was never one to back out of a fight. The siege ended when the building caught fire and both men died.

The danger of war on the horizon led to a London company taking on an insurance policy from a master of a foxhunt. He insured his hunt in the case of invasion and the risk of the men working for the hunt being called up for military service.

The danger of invasion during the First World War was not one that was feared as much as it had been in the Napoleonic Wars. The news of the war, when it eventually came, was received with calm. Trafalgar Square, Whitehall, Parliament Street and Square were filled with people on 5 August waiting for news of whether the British demands on Germany were to be met at midnight. When the war was announced, the crowd began cheering and singing and this went on for twenty minutes before they sang the national anthem. Outside Buckingham Palace the police inspector on duty passed the news of the declaration of war through the railings to the waiting crowds. He told them that Germany had declared war on Britain. He then corrected this to Britain declaring war on Germany. The news spread through the crowd and the cheering led to an appearance by the royal family on the balcony of the palace.

Lord French inspects the troops of the new citizen army as they march past in Hyde Park.

The Americans never arrived until later in the war, but they were welcomed on the streets of London.

Lord Kitchener was to become one of the foremost figures in the military organisation of the army in the First World War.

Men at home eager to get into the war as these crowds trying to enlist shows. This recruiting office was in Whitehall.

The gaiety of the news of war on the night it was declared faded a little the next day. In Whitehall an Irishman was very offended by being mistaken for a German. Then fighting broke out and mounted police had to be called in to control the crowds. Despite the poor weather (it was raining heavily), crowds still hung around the streets. Those in the right place saw the king arrive at the admiralty.

One unexpected result of the outbreak of war was a sudden rush by the population to stock up with food. Many shops in London were soon running low on goods as people began to panic-buy. There was a worry that shortages of food would lead to a rise in prices. Also, while London had been used to seeing queues outside theatres and music halls, now the queues were outside recruitment offices. Cars carried posters to encourage volunteers and all classes of men answered the call. When Hamilton Gibbs went to volunteer, he said that every recruiting centre in London looked as though it had a four-hour queue. He finally managed to enlist and was sent to Woolwich Cavalry depot. Being a member of the upper class he was surprised at his fellow cavalrymen who formed the rank and file. They had shirts sticking out of threadbare trouser seats and toes showing through holes in their boots. Most slept naked and had not had a bath for some time. The war was to be the opportunity for all classes to become better acquainted with each other – though this was not always an advantage.

New Zealand Contingent passing the Law Courts London

1915 - 1918.

Men from New Zealand arrive to swell the ranks of those ready to fight for the old country.

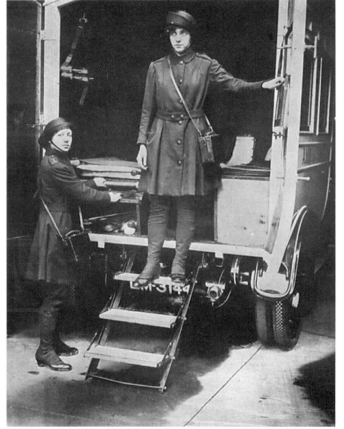

Women were called on to play their part in the war effort in a number of occupations. These women were manning an ambulance.

Territorial camps sprang up in London with men drilling in open spaces such as Temple Gardens. The courtyard of Somerset House became the home of one of the rifle volunteer groups. One of the more popular drill grounds was Hyde Park, which was often full of men drilling both in and out of uniform. In the north of the country there were a number of privately formed battalions, which were paid for by private money. These were the famous pals' battalions, many of which were decimated during the Battle of the Somme. London, however, also had its own special battalions formed by private means. They tended to include men of a higher class than the pals' battalions. One of these was in fact a public schools battalion. There were even plans to have companies within the battalion formed from the old boys of certain schools, such as the Eton Company.

Another privately formed battalion was the Sportsman's Battalion, whose members were men from the world of sport and entertainment. Due to their background, these men were allowed to join up to the age of forty, which was older than the normal upper age limit for those in the ranks. There were some members whose ages were thought to have been nearer sixty but these older men never made it to the front line. Being from such illustrious backgrounds, the recruits for units such as the Sportsman's Battalion would not have enlisted at the normal recruiting office. Their recruiting centre was at the Hotel Cecil, which was at one point the largest hotel in Europe. Whereas normal recruits would also receive a bounty when joining, the sportsmen were asked to make a contribution towards the battalion funds when enlisting.

As with many other new units, the Sportsman's Battalion did their early training in Hyde Park.

The Hotel Cecil was to become one of the more upmarket recruitment centres during the First World War.

When the Sportsman's Battalion left London for their new camp in Essex the crowds turned out to watch them march to Liverpool Street station.

By the end of August recruiting in London was going very well and the patriotic fervour did not appear to be running out of steam. The daily numbers recruited in London in late August and early September were:

August	26	1,725
	27	1,650
	28	1,780
	29	1,800
	30	1,928
	31	1,620
September	1	4,600
	2	4,500
	3	3,600
	4	4,023

Officers were recruited from the public school boys who usually had experience of cadet corps at their schools. Even if they had no experience, those from that class were expected to make better officers. The upper classes would no doubt already have the contacts that would make their transformation to officers easy.

The Junior Army and Navy Club was situated opposite Horse Guards and the War Office. It was also only one minute's walk from the Admiralty and there was a membership fee of seven guineas for those living in London and five guineas for those living outside, meaning that only the better off would be a member.

The Royal Horse Guards found themselves in a different role as they trained to take part in the war on a London golf course.

The Junior Army and Navy Club was close to the centre of army life at Horse Guards. This gave its members access to those in influence in the forces.

There was a common belief that the lower classes expected to be led by officers from the upper classes. There was a saying that the men from the ranks would follow a gentleman to hell and, in many cases, they did just that. The common literature of the time, such as boys' comics, often had heroes who came from the upper classes, but they would usually have a loyal aide who came from the working class and who would have given their life for their master. It all helped to reinforce the belief in gentlemen as officers.

There were early developments in relation to the war and the military. The railways were taken over by the War Office immediately and numerous factories began to produce war-related items, including munitions. In some cases there weren't even factories. In Taylor's book *Jellied Eels and Zeppelins*, she remembers her mother working in a field behind their flat in Walthamstow where mustard gas shells were made in tents.

The increased involvement of the military in everyday life led to the public expecting to see guards at the London stations, but they were disappointed. There were guards, however, on bridges around the edges of London and these men often had a tent pitched by the bridge to live in. However, it wasn't only soldiers who guarded the bridges. At the outbreak of war Sir Robert Baden Powell, the Chief Scout, mobilised his Boy Scout movement and had an army of 20,000 boys in the London area alone. As well as guarding bridges and telegraph lines, the Scouts were used to hand out leaflets, as dispatch riders, and helped families whose men were away. The War Office and police asked for 2,000 Scouts and those involved in war work were excused school attendance.

Even before the war began in August 1914, questions were being asked in the press about the aliens in the country. A bill was passed in the commons giving the government the power to restrain the movement of undesirable aliens. However, what an undesirable alien was had very unclear definitions. Some people – in fact quite a lot of people – saw anyone with connections to those countries on the enemy side in the coming war as undesirable. There were some who saw all

Men from overseas flocked to London to help in the war. These men were from Canada and aroused public interest as they marched through the city.

foreigners as dangerous. While the bill was being reported in the newspapers it was also stated that twenty-one spies had been arrested in the previous twenty-four hours. One group of Germans who left the country quickly were those from the German Embassy. As they left, the plaque was removed from the wall outside the building.

The steps taken were not enough for large numbers of the public and also a number of politicians. There were to be continued debates in the press and in parliament as to what should happen to those seen as enemy aliens. The government stuck by its beliefs for some time and refused to undertake widespread internment of all hostile aliens for which it was widely criticised.

There were a number of foreigners already in London at the outbreak of the war but soon more began to arrive. There were to be large numbers of Belgian refugees fleeing the fighting in their country and there were also a lot of American citizens arriving from Europe where many had been on holiday. Some of these had only just managed to get off of the Continent with the clothes they were wearing. It is believed that there were as many as 20,000 American citizens in London and an office was opened in the Savoy Hotel to help them. There seems to have been quite a scramble by them to get out of England – perhaps they expected the country to be invaded. Even the ones who had money were in difficulties as it wasn't easy to change paper money or travellers' cheques due to the war. Eventually a ship full of gold was sent over from America to help the situation.

The Post Office Rifles training for the war. Although a London regiment they were training in Sussex.

The officers of the 2/8th City of London Battalion, the Post Office Rifles. Their headquarters were at 130 Bunhill Road.

Once the war began, the persecution of Germans living in London increased. The German consul from Sunderland was arrested in London and arms belonging to Germans were seized in Chancery Lane. A German waiter at the Hyde Park Hotel was arrested with a Winchester rifle and maps. In May 1915, anti-German riots broke out in the East End of London. These events were also taking place in many other parts of the country, inspired by air raids from German airships. By 14 May, the riots had begun to tail off during the day, although this was mainly due to the fact that there were no more alien-owned businesses to attack. The numbers involved in the violence were enormous and often included crowds of thousands of people. Special constables were drafted in to the area to help deal with the problem. However, it seems that the police were either powerless to act against such large groups or did little out of sympathy for the reasons behind the attacks. Whatever the reasons, most of those who were arrested were charged with assault on the police rather than with damaging property or attacking enemy aliens. One unexpected result of the attacks was that it became very difficult to get bread in the East End. This was because the majority of baker's shops had been run by foreigners and these had all been attacked and badly damaged and had subsequently gone out of business.

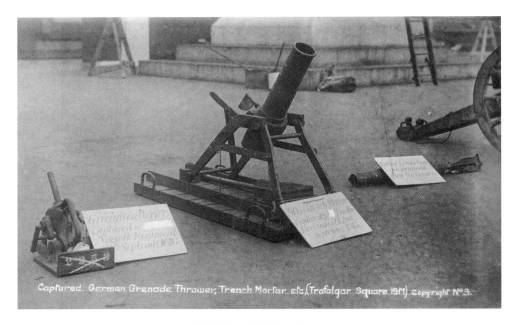

Captured German Grenade Thrower, Trench Mortar etc.(Trafalgar Square 1917) copyright N°3.

A display of captured German weapons in Trafalgar Square.

Many soldiers were billeted in people's homes. This card shows two soldiers in the garden of the house they were occupying in Stoke Newington.

The Artists Rifles wearing strange headgear in a mock-up of a tank. The marked speed of 3 miles per week shows how reliable the tanks were at the time. This may have been a fund raising event.

Other men also began to arrive in London from Europe; the first wounded from the British forces in France. There were soon 300 of them in the Royal London Hospital in Whitechapel, and they were visited by George V and his queen on 3 September 1914. The newspapers reported that all the soldiers who could stiffened to attention as the royal couple entered their wards. Many of the soldiers forgot that they were unable to salute and tried to anyway. A large crowd also gathered outside to see the king and queen as they left.

Hospitals in London were very busy during the war with a large increase in patients owing to the arrival of the wounded. In 1915, 157,510 patients were treated in London hospitals. Of this number, 28,645 were naval or military patients. In 1916 there were 153,512 patients and 27,328 were non-civilian. A number of large buildings in the capital were transformed into hospitals. One of these was the Fulham workhouse and the 900 inmates were spread around other workhouses in the city to make room for the wounded.

The Royal Victoria Patriotic School in Wandsworth had been opened by Prince Albert to house 300 girls orphaned as a result of the Crimean War. It became the 3rd London General Hospital during the war. It began the war with 520 beds, by 1916 there were 1,637 and eventually it rose to 1,800. Apart from the building itself, marquees were used in the grounds and, later, wooden huts were built to accommodate the increased number of beds. One of the sisters at the hospital writing in the *Hospital Gazette* mentioned how convoy after convoy of wounded men would arrive at the hospital both night and day. There was even

Numerous buildings were pressed into service as hospitals. The 3rd London General Hospital in Wandsworth had previously been a school.

Entertaining the wounded men at the 3rd London General Hospital took many forms, such as this wrestling match.

The Hospital through Different Eyes.

There never was a truer saying than "It all depends upon the point of view."

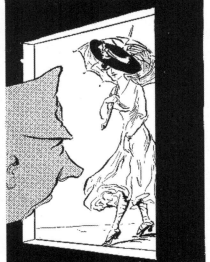

1. The Late Comer (12.30 a.m.): "For narrow is the way——!"

2. The Gate Policeman from his box: "So near and yet so far!"

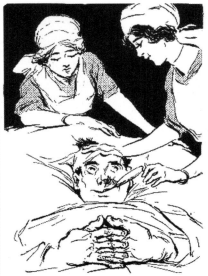

3. The Patient: "Ministering Angels!"

4. The Orderly: "Unrelenting Nemesis!"

Patients at the hospital sent contributions to the Hospital Gazette *of the 3rd London General, such as this cartoon.*

St Dunstan's Hostel in Regent's Park was where those men blinded in the war could learn how to live with their affliction.

a temporary railway station opened outside the hospital to make the transport of the wounded easier. Another story in the *Gazette* was no doubt a piece of propaganda to make the wounded feel better. It told of the case of a man who arrived at the hospital with a bullet wound in his arm. He was seen by a doctor who told him that he could cure the wound. The man had a great deal of money so he decided to see a specialist in Harley Street instead. When he was shown into the doctor's office it turned out to be the same doctor he had seen at the hospital who would have treated him there for nothing.

One of the major forms of training for the new armies was trench-digging. There seemed to have been lots of trench-digging and bayonet fighting practice as this was a cheaper form of training that did not waste scarce supplies such as bullets that rifle practice would have caused. To kill two birds with one stone, the trench-digging was amalgamated into a defensive plan for London. This involved a series of stop lines between the coast and the capital. These were mainly trenches but there were also some pillboxes. The defence of the city again became an important subject at this time and a series of trenches were dug to protect the city but at

A type of incendiary bomb that was dropped in London.

GERMAN INCENDIARY BOMB DROPPED ON LONDON.
Burnt-out shell of a Zeppelin bomb dropped on London. Bound round with tarred rope, it contained a charge which developed terrific heat.

some distance from it, out in the surrounding counties. In Essex the defences also took in the late nineteenth century redoubt at North Weald.

The real threat to London during the war was from the air and the raids by Zeppelins. The first year of the war saw little in the way of raids on the city. The Germans were at first reluctant to use the airships in indiscriminate attacks on civilians. This began to change in 1915 and, although the targets may have supposedly been military and industrial, the inaccuracy of the bombing led to civilian deaths. Special constables were recruited to help deal with the air raid danger. More than 15,000 volunteers had tried to join in the first few weeks of the war and the number of 20,000 needed was soon reached. The first air attack on London was in May 1915 and the Zeppelins then continued their attacks almost unscathed as anti-aircraft fire and British fighter planes were as good as useless in bringing down the airships. By 1917 there were 200 anti-aircraft guns and 300 searchlights based around London. There were also a number of airfields but most of these only lasted for the wartime period.

The actual damage and fatalities caused by the Zeppelin raids were relatively light and also infrequent. The fear that they caused, however, was another matter. This was not helped by the fact that there were no underground shelters in the city, apart of course from the underground railway.

It was not to be until September 1916 that the tide began to turn against the German airmen. A young pilot from Hornchurch airfield in Essex fired a number of new incendiary bullets into the airship *SL11*, causing it to burst into flames and fall out of the sky. The event took place in the skies over London and many of the population saw the fight and cheered as the ship fell to earth, landing at

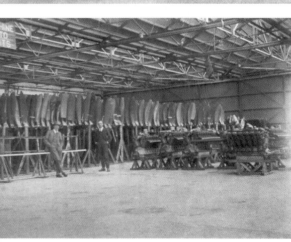

Top left: *The RAF had stores for aircraft and parts in London. This one was at Edgware Road and was known as No. 3 London Stores Distributing Park. It seems that the family of one of the workers took the chance to be in a plane.* Top right: *The workers in the stores seemed to be civilians as this photo shows.* Bottom left: *There were an enormous amount of propellers kept in the stores.* Bottom left: *This photo seems to show how aircraft were transported. This one is fixed to the back of a lorry with its wings detached.*

American troops marching past the Houses of Parliament.

Cuffley. The pilot involved was Lieutenant William Leefe Robinson who became an overnight celebrity. His face graced numerous publications and postcards and he was presented with the Victoria Cross by the king. He also received a large cash prize that had been offered to the first person to bring down a Zeppelin over land. More importantly, his feat was repeated by two more pilots, strangely from the same airfield, soon after.

By the beginning of 1916, other foreigners had begun to arrive in London. These were soldiers from Australia who had come to fight for the old country. According to *The Times* of 6 January 1916 these men were themselves in danger when they arrived in London. The soldiers often came from country districts and were unused to large cities. They were frequently approached by women with the worst possible reputations. The danger of being robbed by these women

Troops setting up a captured German naval gun for public display. The building in the background looks like Horse Guards.

led to suggestions of warning posters being displayed in the trains bringing the men to London. The problem was discussed by a well-known character in a letter to *The Times*. Sir Arthur Conan Doyle called for help in holding in check these vile women who preyed on soldiers. A special constable had told Conan Doyle that these women carried off soldiers to their rooms where they got them drunk and often passed on diseases. Another criticism that Conan Doyle had was that museums had been closed but that brothels had been left open. If it were not for the Union Jack Club and the YMCA, foreign soldiers would return to their country with memories of the most disreputable aspects of London life.

Although there were still some Zeppelin raids in 1917, the first aeroplane raids also began. They were deadlier and much more accurate than their large, unwieldy predecessors. On 13 June 1917 there were raids on London and Kent that led to 162 dead and 432 injured. This included children in an east London school.

Towards the end of the year a number of raids by Gotha bombers were being reported in the newspapers. The claim was, however, that many of the raids did not reach London but were turned back by anti-aircraft fire over Kent and Essex. This was obviously not the complete truth. In 1917 a troop train was just pulling out of Liverpool Street station when a Zeppelin dropped bombs on the

British submarines moored on the Thames with London Bridge in the background.

A scene of Thames Embankment during an air raid. Searchlights light up the sky in the search for the enemy.

Another view of an air raid, this time over Trafalgar Square.

One of the ways that air raid warnings were given in the First World War.

station causing serious injuries to a number of people from flying glass from the station's roof. At a meeting of the Education Committee of the London County Council in January 1918, it was reported that six schools had been hit in raids over two days. There were, then, obviously a number of raids getting through. The collection of souvenirs from these raids was a popular pastime with younger people. Although collections of shrapnel were popular in the Second World War even items such as shards of glass from windows broken in a raid were collectable during the First World War.

The Home Office produced a leaflet giving instructions on what to do during air raids. The leaflet was not widely distributed, however, as it had to be applied for. Some of the instructions may seem obvious now but it should be remembered that the idea of air raids on civilians was a new thing. It stated that no one should listen to rumours of air raids. They should only seek cover if given an official warning, heard anti-aircraft fire or heard bombs dropping. They should not stay in the open but get into a building. Once inside they should stay on the lower floors and not go near a window. If it was not possible to get inside, they should lay on the ground, in a ditch or even behind a tree. It did not explain how one was supposed to know which side of a tree that the bomb may fall on.

There were other changes that took place throughout the war. When Frank Richards came home on leave from France in June 1915, Victoria station was open to the public while soldiers were leaving on trains for the first leg of their journey to France. He remembered groups of people seeing off their men folk and singing and dancing on the platforms. Later in the war, barriers were erected to keep the public off the platforms when leave trains were arriving or leaving to return to France.

When men got to France they were warned about having sexual contact with local women due to the risk of contracting sexually transmitted diseases. Richards remembered that there were also a number of women soliciting outside Victoria station as the soldiers arrived or were about to leave. They were not warned about them, however.

Hamilton Gibbs had a different view of the women in London when he arrived home on leave in 1916. He mentioned how there were now so many women wearing a variety of different uniforms for all the new organisations that had been formed. He also mentioned how the city was now subject to a blackout in the evening due to the air raids.

The end of the war was celebrated by the firing of maroons. Many of the population, however, thought that this was another air raid warning and went to the shelters, cellars, underground stations and anywhere else they were likely to find shelter. It soon became clear what the real meaning was and everyone came out onto the streets again. This included the men from nearby army camps and anyone in uniform was greeted as a hero. Bonfires were lit in Trafalgar Square from whatever materials could be found. The Ministry of Munitions held a firework party in Hyde Park to celebrate victory and they invited all Londoners through the evening newspapers. The display went on for five evenings. Meanwhile, the London Depot of the Army Service Corps held a torchlight procession in Hampstead.

The end of the war may have been a release for the men from the hell of the trenches but what they found at home wasn't always much better. If they escaped the curse of Spanish 'Flu which was killing as many people as had died in the war, then many of them were without work. Many of the men who had given so much found themselves as good as begging. They sold small leaflets in pubs and even went around the streets singing to raise a few pennies.

Part of the victory parade after the war. There are tanks crossing Westminster Bridge.

Naval detachments passing Hyde Park Corner as part of the victory parade.

The cover of a programme for the victory parade on 5 July 1919.

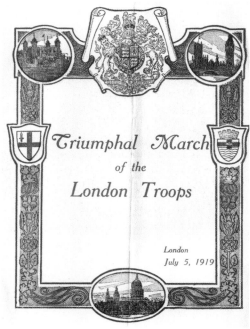

The first page of the victory parade programme. The programme gave the order of march of those taking part.

Part of Germany was occupied by the British Army after the war while the Allies occupied other parts. The London Division was part of the army of occupation and was issued with this guide.

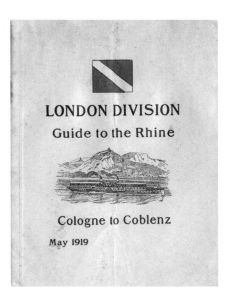

The body of the unknown warrior on its way to Westminster Abbey in November 1920.

After the war, Fenian attacks on London occurred again. One casualty was Sir Henry Wilson who had been Chief of Imperial Staff during the war. He was also an Irish MP who had been an opponent of Republicanism. In 1922 he was on his way home from Liverpool Street station, where he had unveiled a war memorial plaque, when he was shot dead by Reginald Dunn and John Sullivan. They were both caught after a long chase and were executed.

The burial ceremony of the unknown warrior in Westminster Abbey.

It was after the First World War that memorials began to appear in many of the towns in the country. Before this they had been quite rare. This is the Guards' Memorial opposite Horse Guards Parade.

The Machine Gun Memorial at Hyde Park Corner.

The Artillery Memorial at Hyde Park Corner.

The period between the wars may have been one of peace but military matters were never far from the minds of many people. In January 1926 there was a meeting at the Mansion House to discuss the question of transferring units of the Territorial Army from the county to the City of London. The lord mayor presided over a meeting of the London Territorial Army Association. The War Office had suggested that the transfer should take place of the whole of the 56th (1st London) Division to the control of the City of London. No decision was reached on the matter, however.

There was another form of violence that appeared in the years before the Second World War when football hooliganism began to be a problem. Having said that, there had been reported cases of violence between rival football supporters from as early as the 1890s. One club which had been associated with problems of violence was Millwall, whose ground was closed for the first two weeks of the season in 1934 because of crowd trouble in a game against Bradford in March that year.

11

THE SECOND WORLD WAR

Although it is often said that Britain was not prepared for war when it began in 1939, this was not the case in all areas. There had been air exercises from the 1920s where mock air raids had been staged and fighters had been scrambled to intercept the bombers. During an exercise in 1931 there was a squadron of interceptor fighters on duty. The defensive view was that enemy bombers would be spotted crossing the coast. These would either be spotted by those watching for them or heard if they were above the clouds or it was dark. The height and speed would then be worked out and the fighters sent to intercept them.

There were beliefs in some areas that some kind of ray had been developed that would stop enemy aircraft by making their engines cut out before the crossed the coast. These ideas may have come from misguided rumours and ideas of how radar worked, which was in the process of being developed and still top secret. There was also the use of radio waves from the Alexandra Palace, which had been used for early television broadcasting. Television had been abandoned for the wartime period and the radio waves were turned to war use and went some way towards confusing German pilots.

Preparations for air raids had been the duty of local councils which had to submit air raid precaution schemes for government approval from 1937 onwards. These schemes were then being put into operation from 1938. The use of attacks by aircraft was seen as a strong likelihood. It had happened in the First World War and in other conflicts. The expected fatalities from air raids had been vastly overinflated by the air staff based on their views of the raids in the Spanish Civil War; they expected the casualties to number in the thousands every night.

The responsibility for public air raid shelters was left to local councils. Industries had to provide their own shelters for their workers. London was divided into nine groups to deal with the threat of air raids. Groups one to five were for the inner London area and six to nine were the London areas of Kent, Essex, Surrey and Middlesex. As well as dealing with the after-effects of exploded bombs, each

AN AIR RAID
BY NIGHT

BEING A
DISPLAY
BY THE

LONDON UNITS OF THE
1st ANTI-AIRCRAFT DIVISION
TERRITORIAL ARMY

Commander :
Major-General R. H. D. TOMPSON, C.B., C.M.G., D.S.O.

THE defence of London against Air Attack is the responsibility of the Royal Air Force, together with the Anti-Aircraft Groups of the Territorial Army.

This Display is an impression of an air raid by night. Warning is received from a distance. The alarm is given and the guns and searchlights enter the arena. The searchlights pick up the enemy raiders and the guns engage with good effect.

The London Anti-Aircraft Groups require recruits. Any man who is interested in the defence of London is invited to ask for particulars of service at the Territorial Army Association Publicity Stand or from Headquarters, 26th (London) Anti-Aircraft Group, Duke of York's Headquarters, Chelsea, S.W.3.

UNITS TAKING PART :

51st ANTI-AIRCRAFT BRIGADE, R.A., T.A.,
Duke of York's Headquarters, Chelsea, S.W.3.

52nd ANTI-AIRCRAFT BRIGADE, R.A., T.A.,
Duke of York's Headquarters, Chelsea, S.W.3.

26th ANTI-AIRCRAFT SEARCHLIGHT
BATTALION, R.E. (L.E.E.),
Duke of York's Headquarters, Chelsea, S.W.3.

1st ANTI-AIRCRAFT DIVISIONAL SIGNALS, T.A.,
56, Regency Street, Westminster, S.W.1.

LONDON ARMY FIELD ORDNANCE WORKSHOP, T.A.,
Duke of York's Headquarters, Chelsea, S.W.3.

Air raid precautions were in place before the war began. This advertisement was from the Royal Tournament in 1936.

group had an allocated bomb disposal unit from the Royal Engineers to deal with those bombs that failed to detonate. Unexploded bombs were categorised A to D – A being those causing most disruption (i.e. on busy roads or railway lines) and D being those in open country.

Emergency centres were manned twenty-four hours a day once the war began to coordinate services.

Just before the war started, attacks by Fenians began again, with the central electricity offices in Southwark being bombed in 1939. There were also attacks in Harlesden and Brimsdown, Tottenham Court Road, Leicester Square station and King's Cross station.

They weren't the only home-grown enemy to cause violence in the capital. In Cable Street in the East End, Oswald Mosley and his fascist blackshirts were stopped when they tried to march through the area which was occupied by large numbers of Jews. They were held back by the local people, Jews, communists and the dockers.

On 23 August 1939 the London region headquarters of the Civil Defence was manned on a twenty-four hour basis for the first time. The evacuation of expectant mothers, children and cripples from London had already begun. There was also a large evacuation of government officials and civil servants to other parts of the country. Also in place were plans to move the government itself if things got too dangerous in the capital. On 1 September the BBC shut down its fledgling television service. Another London institution became involved in the wartime preparations when the precincts of the Tower of London were declared a prohibited area. The beach below the tower, which had been used as a playground for children, was closed by removing the ladder giving access.

Around 50 per cent of London's children were evacuated with a great deal of effect on the rest of the country. Many of the children from the slums of the city were not as well brought up as those whose homes they arrived in. H.G. Wells said of evacuation that it spread disease, bad habits and unsanitary practices throughout the country. One in six children from London had head lice and there were also large numbers of children with scabies and impetigo. The poor health of so many children showed how bad conditions were in London.

Although it is often said that the war and evacuation led to the classes drawing together, in many cases the arrival of working class children in middle class homes had the opposite effect; especially as there had been no bombing at first. Many of the better off people found the idea of having working class people in their homes abhorrent. Not only were the working class suffering in these situations; minority groups such as Jews often found themselves severally discriminated against in rural areas where such minority groups did not exist.

As the schools in London closed, three-quarters of them were requisitioned by civil defence groups. Many of those children left in London had some home teaching. It has been said that anti-social behaviour increased due to the number of children released onto the streets. In fact, by the beginning of November a number of schools reopened as children returned from their evacuation.

It was not only children and other groups of people that were evacuated from the city. The paintings from the National Gallery were also moved, a wise precaution as they were, of course, irreplaceable. At first the large paintings were sent to Penrhyn Castle in Wales while the smaller paintings were sent to the National Library at Aberystwyth. All the paintings were later moved to an old slate quarry with large underground caverns, also in Wales.

As in the First World War, the thought of enemy aliens being allowed to stay at liberty in the country was regarded with horror by many members of the public and politicians. The difference in regards to the First World War was that the government knew all about foreign people in the country. Although it is often thought that Britain opened its doors to countless refugees from Nazi Germany, this is not quite the case. Between 1919 and 1939 the only refugees allowed into the country were servants and professionals. Those with no money had only one way into the country, which was into a camp run by the Central Council for Jewish Refugees in Kent. Most of these people were intended for further emigration, mainly to America. Refugees who did enter the country were subject to stringent checks so the government were well informed of their presence. This did not stop those opposed to enemy aliens remaining at large calling for internment. In fact by 1940 only 600 aliens had been interned. Public and political pressure, however, led to the eventual internment of the majority of enemy aliens. This of course included many people who had lived in Britain for several years and even included some who had children fighting for the British forces.

Many of the London hotels and restaurants lost their waiters who were often foreign nationals. The level of internment got to such a ridiculous stage that Italian prisoners of war, who had actually been fighting against Britain, were allowed out of camps to work on farms and other places with a great deal of freedom. Meanwhile Italians who had been living and working in Britain for years and had never done anything against the country were interned.

In the early days of the conflict there was a great effort made to entertain the troops in London. *The Times* reported that the canteen of a London barracks was the scene of a concert in September 1939. The show was compèred by Sonnie Hale and after a singsong led by a military band, there were then songs sung by Miss Jessie Matthews. An even more famous performer appeared at a London barracks in October. Gracie Fields made her first public performance since her illness and the concert was reportedly a great success with the soldiers joining in with Miss Fields' songs.

The greatest danger to the population of London in the early months of the war was the blackout. The number of traffic accidents soared and the number of those who died on the roads, both as pedestrians and those in vehicles, rose.

When de Gaulle arrived in London in June 1940, he said that the population looked indifferent to the war. The streets and parks were full of people and there were queues at the cinemas. This view was reinforced by the American journalist Drew Middleton who wrote that the English saw the war as a series of small personal affronts. There was a radio broadcast by American journalists from London during an air raid. Reporters were placed at certain points in the city to record people going to the shelters during a raid. What they found was that people did not rush off in panic but slowly strolled to the shelters, they even recorded one man who stopped to ask one of the reporters for a light before entering the shelter.

There were signs of the expected danger around, however. Post boxes had layers of gas-detecting paint on top of them. At first around three-quarters of the population carried gas masks. By November and the resulting lack of any action, hardly anyone bothered. Thousands of gas masks were left on London's trains and buses and many more were handed into lost property offices in the first few months after the outbreak of war.

Landmarks such as the statue of Eros in Leicester Square were surrounded by sand bags and large numbers of barrage balloons filled the sky above the city. A number of London taxis were commandeered, painted grey and used as auxiliary fire service vehicles. Large tents were put up to hold the expected air raid casualties that the hospitals could not cope with. These, however, damaged public morale and soon disappeared.

After the evacuation from Dunkirk there were large crowds at Waterloo and Victoria railway stations as people tried to get any information they could on family and friends who had been there, from the returning troops. The soldiers were under orders not to speak about the evacuation so the crowds were wasting their time.

The opinions of many Londoners were recorded by a man named Tom Harrison. He had been annoyed at the public opinions printed in the newspapers at the time of the abdication of Edward VIII and believed that the newspapers had no idea of how to gauge public opinion, so he started the Mass Observation Project. Although this was also run on a quite unscientific basis it did record many interesting memories.

Another research project was begun by the Ministry of Intelligence. The Home Intelligence study was to be used to find out how people were standing up to the expected air raids. It was thought that people in the less affected towns had the higher level of morale, despite the bombing. There are of course other views and it was seen that the occupants of some towns who did not suffer as many raids as London had a much lower level of morale than Londoners who adapted better to the danger, as they suffered it so often.

The first bomb to be dropped close to London was in June 1940 at Addington. On 19 July the Germans dropped the newspaper containing the 'Last Appeal To Reason'. It was a speech by Adolf Hitler that blamed Britain for starting the

Churchill inspecting a Home Guard unit. In the early days of the war, Churchill may have exaggerated how well armed and trained the Home Guard were in order to mislead the Germans.

war. Copies of the paper were sold to raise money for the Red Cross and other good causes or were destroyed. There was speculation in the press in July as to whether London would be declared an open city in the event of invasion, as Paris had been, to stop any further damage. A speech by Churchill answered the question when he declared that, 'Every house and every street of London would be defended to the last.'

A German broadcast in response to Churchill's views described the Home Guard as musketeers armed with shotguns and pitchforks who invited the most terrible reprisals and were no source of strength. In August the Home Guard in South London responded in an astonishing way to this slur. After being machine-gunned by an enemy dive-bomber, the Home Guard unit opened fire on the plane with their rifles and brought it down. The plane, which was flying at about 400ft, was shot at, then the attackers telephoned the next post about three-quarters of a mile away who also opened fire as the plane flew over them. The plane then crashed.

The first raids on London began in August 1940 – before this the raids had been concentrated on the RAF airfields. The bad news for London was, however, good news for the RAF. If raids on the airfields had continued then the RAF would have been much less successful in fighting the Germans in the air. The Germans made a further mistake when they shifted a large part of their air force to attack

The Cabinet War Rooms, now a museum open to the public.

Russia when Londoners were beginning to feel as though it could not take much more. Not only were air raids common by the end of August, so were dogfights in the skies above the city. The raids on London were to carry on consistently until November. The worst sufferers were those in the East End, although raids on the West End did increase later. Although the position of bombs dropped was not reported in the newspapers – as it gave the Germans evidence of where their raids had been successful – the position of downed German aircraft seems to have

Messages to show how people were carrying on as normal were common, as can be seen here.

While road traffic was often disrupted by the bombing, river transport helped Londoners to cope.

Just as in the First World War the streets of London found themselves visited by men from overseas who had come to fight the enemy. A London policeman directs these visitors from New Zealand.

The fires caused by bombing had to be prioritised by the fire service as they could not cope with them all.

Firefighting did not only take place on the streets as this river scene shows.

been. On 16 September there were photographs in the newspapers of a German Dornier aircraft that had been brought down by Victoria station.

It was not only the evacuation that showed the difference between classes during the war. Not only did the people of the East End suffer from the heaviest raids, they also had to put up with the worst shelters. However, many of the down and outs in the city had their own shelters at the Hungerford Club, based in railway arches at Charing Cross station. It was run by the Anglican Pacifist Fellowship, although these shelters did not compare with those such as at the Dorchester. Their shelter was a converted Turkish bath with beds covered with eiderdowns and with dressing gowns hanging above them.

The city was not ready for what was to come. Before September 1940, 80 per cent of the Auxiliary Fire Service had never fought a fire. They were soon, however, thrown into the forefront of danger, fighting incendiaries, often as other bombs dropped around them. There were not enough firefighters to deal with every fire and difficult decisions had to be made as to which fires to ignore – there was no point in trying to fight or save buildings that were completely burnt out. The service quickly gained the experience to concentrate on fighting those fires that might spread and treat all attacks on a district basis rather than an individual level. Things began to improve by early 1941 when many members of the public fought incendiary fires as well as the firemen themselves.

It was not only the emergency services that put themselves in danger to help. When gas mains were fractured by bombs the men from the gas boards often had to fight their way through burning buildings in order to turn off the gas supply, putting themselves in danger to help save others from potentially dangerous explosions.

One memory of the raids was given to the Mass Observation Project by Frank Edwards. During a raid on 25 September 1940 he explained how he went to the cellar of his house. They could hear bombs dropping and anti–aircraft guns that one minute sounded close, the next further away. When Edwards went to check he found some broken windows in his house. What was interesting was Edwards' memories of the following morning. Of course, no one knew what they would find – or not find – when they came out of the shelter. He found that the houses on his side of the street had windows broken at the back. Those on the opposite side, however, had the windows broken at the front. He also found that the shops round the corner had broken windows and their stock was spread across the road by the bombs.

Damage to shops often led to signs of defiance appearing. Broken shop windows were often a reason to display signs saying 'More Open Than Normal'. Public houses with no glass left in the windows would often advertise themselves with slogans such as 'Windows Gone But Our Spirits Are Excellent'.

The Germans were quick to capitalise on the situation in London and were not averse to exaggerating the situation for their own population's benefit. A German radio broadcast of 3 October 1940 stated that, 'London was facing riots, the authorities proved to be helpless and everywhere there is the greatest confusion.' There were some devastating raids on the city, however. On 29 December 1940,

Left: *Searching the rubble for casualties after a raid could be an upsetting and gory task.*
Right: *No buildings were immune to attack as the damage to St Thomas' Hospital shows.*

Among the historic buildings damaged by the bombing was the library and hall of the Inner Temple.

When the Houses of Parliament were damaged by bombing, use was made of the rubble. These bricks were turned into souvenirs and sold in aid of the Red Cross.

Left: *The washing still had to be done even if the house was falling down around you.*
Right: *The mail had to be delivered as long as the post boxes were still standing.*

1,436 people died and 1,792 were seriously injured in a single raid that covered all of London. Buildings such as the Tower of London, Westminster Abbey and the British Museum were hit – 750,000 books from the museum were destroyed.

The wardens' work not only took place during the raids, but would also go on the next day as they searched the ruins for survivors. Local knowledge was of vital importance, as wardens often knew if local families were in shelters, at home or somewhere else. There was little point searching the wreckage of a house if the family always went to public shelters during raids. The aspect of the work of the air raid wardens that was not publicised was how they were expected to collect baskets of flesh after raids. It was only if enough parts of a body were found that they were taken to the mortuary. They would often let the families of the dead think that the bodies were complete but many of the dead were never found and some members of the public saw the real results when they came out of shelters after a raid discovering for themselves parts of bodies lying in the street – the bodies of those who did not make it to the shelters in time. This horrible job was often performed by the Military Pioneers who were mainly foreigners, many of whom had been interned as enemy aliens early in the war. Many of the activities they performed took place behind screens to save the scenes of carnage being witnessed by the public.

The view that the population stood up well to the bombing was not entirely true of those who suffered the most. The East End around the docks came in for the heaviest bombing of the war and not everyone sat around the piano singing and daring Hitler to do his worst, which is the popular view of the cheery cockney. Parts of West Ham became almost a ghost town as many of the population moved out and took part in self-inflicted evacuations to the calmer towns further inland, such as Oxford where some colleges became hostels for the people arriving from London. Even Epping Forest became a large camp for those escaping the bombing. The actual population of the East End fell by 50 per cent by 1943. London itself had only 75 per cent of the pre-war population. There were parts of the East End that were so empty that the army used the areas for training in street fighting.

The bad feeling among the population was not only aimed at the Germans. There were also negative attitudes towards the government. Many felt that not enough was being done to help the population. Air raid shelters were inadequate and no one seemed to have planned for the time that would have to be spent in the shelters or the fact that, while in them, people would have to eat, sleep and use a toilet. Another danger associated with raids was the number of unexploded bombs that were left lying around. There were huge numbers of these, which often stopped areas being occupied until they were dealt with. There were even attempts by the government to stop the public using the London Underground as a shelter, which seemed a strange idea when they would have seemed to be

In May 1941 the Royal Dutch Army Band was the first band to march through London since the war began.

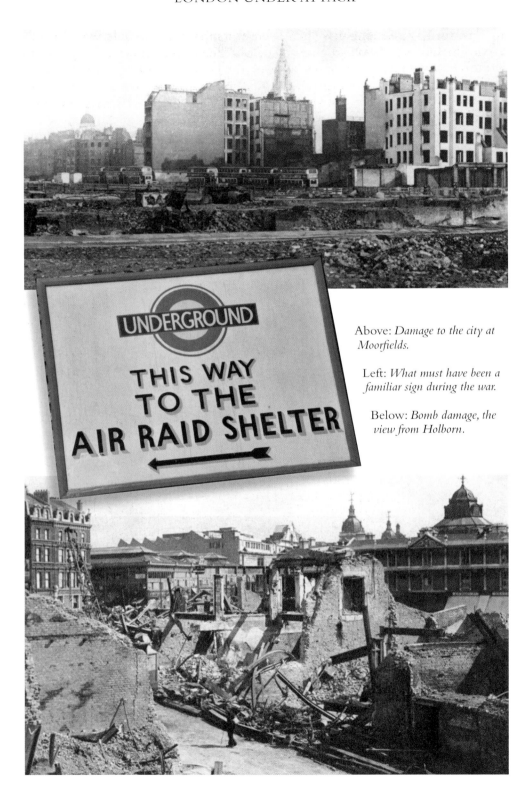

Above: *Damage to the city at Moorfields.*

Left: *What must have been a familiar sign during the war.*

Below: *Bomb damage, the view from Holborn.*

an ideal ready-made amenity. There were fears that some people would try to live in the Underground and never come out. There were in fact attempts to do just this in some places. A number of caves in Chiselhurst in Kent were occupied as shelters and eventually a thriving underground community developed with people furnishing their own small part of the caves. A special train ran from London every evening taking those who worked in the city home to their families who were living in the caves.

Officially, then, at first the Underground stations were not used as shelters. People got round this by buying platform tickets and sleeping in them anyway. This seems to go against the view that people were getting on with their lives as normal despite the bombing. There were queues for places in stations, which sometimes began in the morning, and touts would sell places in the stations for half a crown. Lines were painted on the platforms and the first line could not be crossed until 7.30 in the evening. The second line could not be crossed until 10.30 which allowed passengers to still get on trains.

The Underground was not completely safe for those sheltering in it. Floodgates had to be added to some stations where the tunnels ran under the Thames in case a bomb led to a leak. Marble Arch station was hit by a bomb, which caused the tiles to fly off the wall hitting people – twenty people died in that incident. The worst incident occurred at Bethnal Green station. It was thought that the sound of anti-aircraft rockets close by led to a panic as people went into the station. One person fell, causing others to fall and 173 people died in the crush.

The Underground was not an entirely unwelcome place for children to shelter as it had many attractions that normal shelters did not have. There were chocolate machines on the platforms and weighing machines where you could see if the

Even the tracks were used to sleep on by those sheltering in the Underground.

chocolate had made you put on weight. Then there were always trains that could be ridden along to other stations and even escalators to ride up and down on.

Overall, the number of people in shelters was quite low. In November 1940 it was estimated that 9 per cent of the population of London slept in public shelters. There were another 4 per cent in the Underground, and 27 per cent in domestic shelters. The rest were either on duty or at home, often sleeping under a table or under the stairs.

One of the most difficult experiences must have been for those working in hospitals who often had to move patients during raids. Some hospitals had basements where emergency wards could be set up. In some cases patients were moved from the top floors to basements every night.

While the trains still ran underground, on the surface things were not as easy. Trams and trolley buses were vulnerable to attacks as parts of the track or the overhead wires being damaged meant that entire routes could be put out of action. Normal motorbuses coped better, but many of these were destroyed as well. The number of familiar red double-deckers was increased by multicoloured reinforcements from other parts of the country.

One of the symbols of survival of the city was the dome of St Paul's Cathedral, which seemed to miraculously defy the German bombs night after night, often while the city burned around it. Churchill ordered that the building be saved at all costs due to its effect on the morale of the London population. The photograph of the dome towering above the smoke of the burning city must be one of the most memorable photographs of the Blitz. The reality of St Paul's survival was not quite so miraculous but more a story of the bravery of a large number of men. While much of the population of the city huddled in shelters, a force of 200 men, including John Betjeman, were at work to save the building from incendiary bombs. The men were often outside on the dome of the building during air raids. One incendiary was pushed off the dome by a member of the watch. St Paul's was hit by one bomb, which destroyed the organ that dated from the seventeenth century.

It was not only in London that the importance of St Paul's was realised. There was a report in the *New York Times* in September 1940 which stated that the United States saluted the brave men who were trying to save St Paul's. They were led by a Lieutenant Davies and risked their lives for a symbol – St Paul's was like a flag flying above the decks of a beleaguered battleship. The flag must not fall while there were Britons to save it!

After the first few years of the war the raids on London tailed off, but they never stopped completely. Even after D-Day there was more to come when in June 1945 the V1s began to fall on the city and there was another wave of evacuation. One of the best remembered of these occurred on 18 June when a V1 fell on the Guards Chapel, where many senior officers were present for a service, killing 119 people. Then the V2s began to arrive in August. Despite the

The enormous American officers' mess at Park Lane.

The Canadian Air Force memorial in Lincoln's Inn Fields.

The building here was the Canadian Air Force headquarters. It was no. 20 Lincoln's Inn Fields.

The Guards' Chapel at Wellington Barracks was one of the sites hit by a V1 in 1944 with a number of high-ranking casualties. The list of names on the wall outside are those from the memorials in the chapel that were destroyed when the bomb struck.

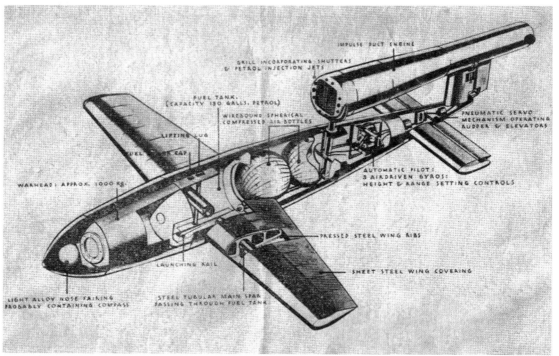

A plan of a V1 flying bomb.

fear that these weapons aroused, they never achieved the same level of damage that the large early raids had caused. The story of one V2 was told to me by Mrs Pam Kox. Pam was a young girl and although she had been evacuated early in the war, she had come back to her home in Chingford soon after. At just after 9 a.m. on the morning of 15 January 1945, Pam was getting dressed in her bedroom when she heard a loud unusual sound, which she described as a thud. She dived under her bed without thinking. A V2 had landed at the junction of Kings Head Hill and Pole Hill Road, just a few hundred yards from Pam's home. The thing that stuck in her mind most about the incident was how long it took for the debris that the bomb had thrown up to fall back to the ground. In one of the strange coincidences that often occur, the families living on the opposite corners of Pole Hill Road were named East and West. Mrs West was one of the fatalities, the number of which were extremely light considering that five houses in Kings Head Hill were completely destroyed. Mrs East on the other side of the road survived as, after seeing her husband off to work, she had gone back to bed in her Morrison shelter. The reason that casualties were so light was probably due to the time that the rocket fell. Most people had already left for work or school so many of the houses were empty. The only other fatality was a young boy of six, Anthony Wood, who was on his way to school with other children. He had stopped to look into a garden, which had ducks and chickens. The other children walked on and were unhurt. The damage to local services meant that the families living in the area had no water, gas or electricity for some time and a mobile emergency feeding unit was set up in the road. The V2 was not Pam's only experience of the bombing. She told me that the sky was often bright red in the evenings, caused by the flames as London burned. The experience of going through such traumas did not turn Pam against the Germans as a people. While working as a student at Hayes Hill Farm she met a German prisoner of war who was also working there. She later married Josef Kox and he stayed in Britain after the war. They lived in the house next door to the one which Pam lived in when the V2 fell.

The amount of damage done to the city by enemy air raids was devastating. One borough of London that was badly hit was Camberwell. It was in fact the fourth-worst bombed area of London during the short period of the flying bombs. There were 190 killed and 734 seriously injured in this stage of the war. The number of houses totally destroyed was 433, and 749 were so seriously damaged that they

Plaque to the 1st Anti-Aircraft Division RASC. It is set in the wall of the Transport Department building in Mile End Road.

147

were beyond repair. More than 4,000 homes were damaged badly enough to take some time to repair and more than 22,000 were slightly damaged.

One famous member of the 5th London Battalion Home Guard, whose headquarters were in St John's Wood, was the writer George Orwell. Because of his experience fighting in the Spanish Civil War and as a former member of the cadet forces at his school, he was made a sergeant. Orwell wrote several articles calling for gun shops to hand out their stocks to the Home Guard. This would have seemed an excellent idea when stocks of weapons were sitting on the shelves while the Home Guard were armed with knives tied to broom handles. Orwell also wanted the government to supply them with grenades. He gave several lectures on street fighting but his views were often overruled by the elderly men in command of most Home Guard units. These men still thought in terms of their service in the First World War or even the Boer War. They wanted the Home Guard to have drilling and bayonet practice and be able to dig trenches.

Apart from the danger of invasion from abroad there was another threat to London. There was a supposed plan to invade the city during the war from an unlikely source; German prisoners of war who were planning to stage mass breakouts from their camps and then march on London. This was after D-Day when the majority of the Allied fighting men had gone to Europe. The plan was supposed to be a way of taking pressure off the Germans under attack on the Continent.

A number of escapes did take place, or were attempted, but it is not clear how serious this threat was. There were also suggestions that German paratroopers would be dropped to help with this plan. This was of course late in the war when the number of German prisoners in Britain was very high. Early in the war, many

HMS Belfast *played a part in D-Day. It is now a floating museum close to Tower Bridge.*

German prisoners were sent to camps in other parts of the Empire, such as Canada. There were a number of reasons for this. One was lack of food to feed large numbers of prisoners, but another was that if the Germans had invaded Britain, the prisoners of war would have been a source of reinforcements for an invasion force.

There was another venue for some notorious German prisoners as well as the many PoW camps. The Tower of London had been a prison throughout history but captives within its walls had been very rare in the recent past. Josef Jacobs was a German spy who had been captured after parachuting into England during the war. Although not held in the tower, he was brought there after his trial to face his sentence of execution. Due to a sprained ankle, Jacobs could not stand and so faced his firing squad sitting down. The sentence was carried out in the East Casement Rifle Range, which was out of view of the public.

Jacobs was not the only German prisoner to be executed in London during the war, although he was the only one executed in the tower. Other prisoners were hanged in London's prisons for attacking and killing fellow prisoners inside their camps. These were often avid Nazis who saw those who were less strong in their support of the party as traitors and dealt with them accordingly. One German prisoner who was held for some time in the Tower of London was Rudolf Hess. Why Hess had parachuted out of his Messerschmitt over Scotland in 1941 was never explained. Hess was treated like one of the more important prisoners of the past that were held in the tower and Churchill told Foreign Secretary Anthony Eden that he should be provided with books, writing materials and recreation. Hess was then moved to a house in Hampshire in 1945.

Crowds gather at Buckingham Palace to celebrate the end of the war.

The statue of Earl Alexander of Tunis at Wellington Barracks. He served with distinction in both world wars.

The end of the war in Europe led to spontaneous celebrations around the country. Those who could, however, got to London where the royal family and Churchill were. The streets were full of people celebrating and a national holiday was announced. As night fell, the city was lit up again and many young children had never seen it like this at night. The streets were not only full of Union Jacks but also the flags of Russia and America. St Paul's Cathedral was packed all day long with people giving thanks for peace. At 3 o'clock Churchill broadcast to the nation and to the crowds outside parliament who heard the speech on loudspeakers. He then made an appearance on a balcony overlooking St James's Park to take the adulation of the crowds, as did the royal family at Buckingham Palace. The joy at the end of the war in Europe was not felt by all, however. There was still fighting going on in the Far East against the Japanese and many of the men out there and their families at home felt that they had been forgotten by those celebrating at home.

It would seem that the end of the war should have led to a period of peace and calm in the capital. This may have been the case for a few years but the sight of crowds engaged in violence on London's streets was to return within a few decades, as were attacks on the population and the armed forces from an old enemy and a new one.

Above left: *The statue of Churchill in Parliament Square.*

Above right: *It is not only those who fought in the war that are commemorated. This plaque set in a large rock in Tavistock Square commemorates conscientious objectors.*

The cover of the programme of the victory celebrations in June 1946. The programme gave the route and the order of march for those taking part.

12

THE POST-WAR PERIOD

In 1958 a new outbreak of violence hit the capital with serious gang violence between newly arrived West Indian immigrants and gangs of Teddy Boys. *The Times* reported that three organisations were watering the ground in the area around Notting Hill where the main trouble occurred. These were Mosley's Union Movement, the National Labour Party – who wanted to ban coloured immigration – and the Britons Publishing Society who published a newsletter called *Black and White News* containing anti-Black articles. The troubles also led to Conservative calls for immigration control.

The trouble attracted those who wanted to be involved in violence against the Black immigrant population. On 16 September at the Old Bailey, nine youths

Guns being fired on the Thames Embankment with Tower Bridge visible through the smoke.

The Territorial Army are still an important part of the British forces. This Territorial Building stands in Handel Street and is the home of the University of London Officer Training Corp.

Many of the soldiers in London have a ceremonial aspect to their duty. The Guards Band is photographed marching into Buckingham Palace.

were imprisoned for four years after being found touring the area of Notting Hill looking for black men to beat up. A number of black men were injured after attacks by the group.

There was obviously seen to still be a need for a certain number of troops to be based in London by 1960 although many barracks in the countryside were closing due to the reorganisation of the army. Even the guards had been reduced from ten to eight battalions. The household troops, however, still needed their three barracks at Chelsea, Knightsbridge and Wellington. The rebuilding of Chelsea barracks had just begun in June 1960 and was not to be completed until 1962. The other barracks were also to be modernised and altogether the three barracks covered 24 acres.

The 1960s also saw the return of terrorism to the capital. In August 1967 there was a machine gun attack on the US embassy in Upper Grosvenor Square. Three men in a white Ford Cortina fired at the building but there were no casualties. A note was later found condemning murder by US soldiers, claiming to be from the Revolutionary Solidarity Movement.

The following year, in March 1968, there was a bomb attack at the Spanish Embassy in Belgravia Square. A bomb was placed against the embassy door but there were again no casualties. A little later another bomb went off at the Columbia Club for US officers at Lancaster Gate. Again there were no casualties.

Guards drilling at Wellington Barracks, a popular sight for tourists.

The cavalry may have lost its function as a fighting force but it is still an attraction for visitors to the capital.

A cavalry unit in the Mall.

The bombs were thought to be the work of a Spanish Anarchist group.

In January 1975 there were two machine gun attacks on London Hotels. The first was on the Captain's Barr restaurant at the Portman Hotel, while a few hours later there was a further attack on the Rib Room restaurant at the Carlton Towers Hotel. Eight people were injured. Both venues were popular with Jewish clientele and an anti-Semitic feeling was thought to be the reason.

In 1978 there was a machine gun attack on an Israeli El Al airline crew, leaving two dead and nine injured. They were on a bus on their way to the Europa Hotel, Mayfair, for a stopover in London. Three men attacked the bus with machine guns and one of them blew himself up with his own grenade.

In June 1982 the Israeli ambassador Shlomo Argov was shot while leaving a dinner at the Dorchester Hotel. The attackers were three Arabs who were pursued by the ambassador's Scotland Yard bodyguard. He shot one of the men himself when threatened with a gun.

In June 1985 a bomb was left outside the Syrian Embassy in Mayfair. The 10lb device was safely detonated. It had been left on the steps of the embassy between 8.00 and 10.00 p.m. and it is thought to have been the work of Palestinian terrorists opposed to the Damascus government.

The violence on the post-war streets did not only come from foreigners. In the late 1960s and early 1970s there was a new youth culture called Skinheads whose favourite pastime was violence. The capital's football grounds were the scenes of tribal violence, which often spilled onto the streets as rival fans fought each other.

Another aspect to the violence carried out by the Skinheads reflected the events of the late 1950s in Notting Hill. This time, however, it was the Asian immigrants who found themselves in the firing line and the youths' new pastime became known as Paki-bashing.

There was a return by the IRA in the 1980s and the suspicion that a Christmas bombing campaign was expected by the IRA in 1980. This was after two bombs exploded at the Territorial Army Hall in Hammersmith Road, occupied by the 31st Signals regiment. One bomb exploded outside the hall and another in a car. Some damage was done to the hall and a few passers by were injured.

In early 1981 there were riots at Brixton, Hackney and Southall, which mainly seemed to involve black youths fighting the police. There were a number of seemingly copycat riots on a smaller scale such as one in Finsbury Park when a gang of a few hundred black youths ran through a funfair throwing stones. The police described the event as just hooliganism.

There were more serious disturbances 1982 when the IRA returned with a number of attacks. There were eight deaths and fifty-three injuries when two bombs exploded in London parks within a few hours of each other. A car bomb in Hyde Park exploded as a squad of household cavalry, the Blues and Royals, were passing on their way to the changing of the guard ceremony. The bomb was made from 10lb of explosives wrapped in nails. Two soldiers were killed, four soldiers and two mounted policemen were wounded along with seventeen members of the public. Seven horses also died.

A little later, a bomb went off in Regent's Park where the band of the Royal Green Jackets had been playing at the bandstand. In this attack six soldiers died and thirty members of the public were injured.

October saw two more attacks when Lieutenant General Sir Stuart Pringle, the commandant general of the Royal Marines, lost a leg when a bomb exploded under his car at his Dulwich home. Kenneth Howard, a bomb disposal officer, was killed defusing a bomb in a Wimpy Bar in Oxford Street while the police defused another bomb in a Debenhams store nearby.

November 1982 saw another two attacks. At Woolwich Barracks two women were injured when a toy gun filled with explosives blew up. Then the Wimbledon home of Sir Michael Havers QC, the attorney general, was also bombed.

In 1990 there were poll tax riots which were often referred to in the same breath as those which had taken place in London so many years before. There was looting and damage to 100 shops and 500 arrests. There were, however, no executions of public figures. There were 500 police injuries and constant debates over police handling of the demonstrations, as there have been of all demonstrations since.

Terrorist attacks were to continue in one form or another as they have at regular intervals since the 1960s. In the 1990s there were further Irish attacks including a mortar attack on 10 Downing Street, and bombs at Victoria, Paddington and the Baltic Exchange.

Since the problems in Ireland have been brought to a peaceful conclusion, the twenty-first century has seen renewed violence, although the enemy has now changed. The most recent attacks in London have been carried out by militant Muslim groups, leading to deaths on the London Underground and on the capital's buses. Also, the number of stabbings of young people on London's streets has increased significantly since so-called 'gang culture' has become the norm.

Whatever one thinks about the violence on the streets of our capital city today, it is clear that there has been nothing new in what goes on. All the forms and reasons for violence have been present in the past and it would seem that history will continue to repeat itself in the future. Comparisons on the levels of violence in different times are, however, futile. It is the personal effect of violence that makes the difference and it would seem that the only certainty is that violence in London is here to stay. Anyone who doubts this should take a stroll around the area of Downing Street and see the policemen now armed with machine guns.

BIBLIOGRAPHY

Abbott, G., *Who's Buried Under Your Floor*, Eric Dobby, 2008

Armstrong, W., *The Thames From Its Rise To The Nore*, Virtue & Co, 1880s

Baker, T., *Medieval London*, Cassell, 1970

Bowle, J. (ed), *The Diary of John Evelyn*, Oxford University Press, 1985

Braddick, M., *God's Fury, England's Fire*, Penguin, 2009

Brandon, D., *Stand And Deliver*, Book Club Associates, 2001

Brooke-Hunt, V., *Prisoners of the Tower of London*, J.M. Dent, 1901

Calder, A., *The People's War*, Pimlico, 1992

Cochrane, Lord Admiral, *Memoirs of a Fighting Captain*, Folio Society, 2005

Collingwood, R.G., *The Archaeology of Roman Britain*, Bracken, 1930

Edwards, F., *The Gunpowder Plot*, Folio Society, 1973

Essex Record Office, T2/561/42/1, *Essex During The French Wars*

Grainge, G., *The Roman Invasions of Britain*, Tempus, 2005

Hamilton Gibbs, A., *Gun Fodder*, Little Brown & Co, 1923

Harrington, P., *English Civil War Fortification 1642–51*, Osprey, 2003

Lloyd, P., *The French are Coming*, Spellmount, 1991

Maurice-Jones, Colonel K.W., *The History of the Coast Artillery in the British Army*, Naval and Military Press

Mail on Sunday, Milton, G., 'A Day In Hitler's London', 19 July 2009

Ministry of Information, *Front Line*, 1942

Morris, M., *Edward I – A Great and Terrible King*, Hutchinson, 2008

Pierce, P., *Old London Bridge*, Review, 2002

Planche, J.R., *Recollections and Reflections, A Professional Autobiography*, Tinsley Brothers, 1872

Richards, F., *Old Soldiers Never Die*, Naval and Military Press

Russell, Lieutenant John, *A Series Of Military Experiments*, Naval and Military Press

Sturdy, D., *Alfred the Great*, Constable, 1995

Swanton, M. (ed), *The Anglo-Saxon Chronicle*, Dent, 1996

Taylor, S., *Jellied Eels and Zeppelins*, Thorogood, 2003

Thornbury, W., *Old and New London*, Cassell, 1890

The Times, 6 February 1917, 7 January 1926, 23 September 1939, 20 October 1939, 20 August 1940, 10 September 1958, 16 September 1958, 29 June 1960, 22 April 1981

Whiting, C., *The March on London*, Leo Cooper, 1996

Wool, A., *The Battle of South London*, Crystal Publications